THE RAPTURE

THE RAPTURE

E. SCHUYLER ENGLISH

LOIZEAUX BROTHERS
Neptune, New Jersey

SECOND EDITION, MAY 1970
FOURTH PRINTING, MAY 1986

Published by LOIZEAUX BROTHERS, INC.
*A Nonprofit Organization, Devoted to the Lord's Work
and to the Spread of His Truth*

Library of Congress Cataloging-in-Publication Data

English, E. Schuyler (Eugene Schuyler), 1899–
    The rapture : an examination of what the Scriptures
teach as to the time of the translation of the church
in relation to the tribulation.

    Previously published as: Re-thinking the rapture.
1954.
    1. Rapture (Christian eschatology) 2. Tribulation
(Christian eschatology) I. Title.
BT887.E54 1986   236   86–7380
ISBN 0–87213–144–0

PRINTED IN THE UNITED STATES OF AMERICA

To

PREFACE

During the past several years there has been a wave of discussion, both in this country and abroad, about the time of the translation of the Church in relation to the period of tribulation that is to come upon this earth as this age draws to its close. The teaching that the Church will not escape the Tribulation but must pass through it has been on the increase. Several books have been published promoting this viewpoint, writings that have been rather widely read. Not a few of God's people have abandoned the doctrine of the pre-tribulation rapture of the Church and have become post-tribulationists. It seems timely, therefore, that this treatise, examining the Scriptures anew on the subject, should be issued.

These studies first appeared in the magazine, *Our Hope*, from October, 1949 to March, 1951. There has been demand for their appearance in book form. So it is that this volume is published in this revised and somewhat enlarged form.

These pages in no way constitute an attack upon anyone but simply a re-examination of certain of the Scriptures that pertain to the subject under discussion, especially those passages in the Bible that have been employed by men who hold views opposed to the pre-tribulation position. Purposely we have omitted, in citations from their writings, the authors' names and the titles of their books, lest personalities should enter that which is not a personal issue but a doctrinal one.

It is our earnest desire that, above all else, this work will serve to quicken in many hearts the expectancy of "that blessed hope, and the glorious appearing of the great God and our Saviour Jesus Christ."

E. S. E.

Skytop, Pa.
November, 1953

TABLE OF CONTENTS

CHAPTER XI

CHAPTER XII

CHAPTER XIII

CHAPTER XIV

CHAPTER XV

"Looking for the blessed hope, and the glorious appearing of the great God and our Saviour Jesus Christ" (Titus 2:13).

CHAPTER I

THE MATTER UNDER DISCUSSION

There are two classes of people to whom the subject that is to be discussed in these pages will be of little interest: those who do not believe that Christ is coming again; and those who hold the view that His return will be after the Millennium. While it is not likely that many that come within either of these classifications will be reading these studies, it may be well, nevertheless, to establish what the Bible has to say about the fact of the return of the Lord Jesus Christ, and to say something about what relation that return has, in time, to the Millennium.

1. The Witness of the Old Testament to the Return of Christ

Not only the New Testament, but the Old as well, gives witness to the return of our Lord Jesus Christ. It is quite true that no such term as "the return of Christ," or "the second coming of the Lord," is to be found in the Old Testament. But neither is Deity described as the Trinity in the Bible. Yet the one is as true as the other.

There are scores of predictions in the Old Testament concerning the throne upon which David's greater Son will reign in peace and righteousness, the coming of the Lord to destroy His enemies, the glorification of Messiah upon His coming to earth, and the like. We cite but a few. Through Nathan the Lord made a covenant with His servant David, the king, saying: "Thine house and thy kingdom shall be established for ever before thee: thy throne shall be established for ever"

(II Sam. 7:16). David himself prophesied in the Holy Spirit concerning Messiah's kingdom, when he wrote the words that Jehovah will one day speak: "Yet have I set My king upon My holy hill of Zion"; and added the Son's reply: "I will declare the decree: the Lord hath said unto Me, Thou art My Son; this day have I begotten Thee." Whereupon the Father answers: "Ask of Me, and I shall give Thee the heathen for Thine inheritance, and the uttermost parts of the earth for Thy possession. Thou shalt break them with a rod of iron; Thou shalt dash them in pieces like a potter's vessel" (Psa. 2:6–9).

Isaiah prophesied: "And there shall come forth a rod out of the stem of Jesse, and a Branch shall grow out of His roots: and the Spirit of the Lord shall rest upon Him . . . and He shall not judge after the sight of His eyes, neither reprove after the hearing of His ears: but with righteousness shall He judge the poor, and reprove with equity for the meek of the earth: and He shall smite the earth with the rod of His mouth, and with the breath of His lips shall He slay the wicked. . . . They shall not hurt nor destroy in all My holy mountain: for the earth shall be full of the knowldege of the Lord, as the waters cover the sea. And in that day there shall be a root of Jesse, which shall stand for an ensign of the people; to it shall the Gentiles seek: and His rest shall be glorious" (Isa. 11:1–3, 9, 10).

Finally, hear the enunciation of Malachi, written in the last chapter of the Old Testament: "For, behold, the day cometh, that shall burn as an oven; and all the proud, yea, and all that do wickedly, shall be stubble: and the day that cometh shall burn them up, saith the Lord of hosts, that it shall leave them neither root nor branch. But unto you that fear My name shall the Sun of righteousness arise with healing in His wings; and ye shall go forth, and grow up as calves of the stall. And ye shall tread down the wicked; for they shall be ashes under the soles of your feet in the day that I shall do this, saith the Lord of hosts" (Mal. 4:1–3).

None of these things occurred when the blessed Son of God became flesh and dwelt among men on this earth for thirty-three years. Yet it is said in the inerrant Word of God that they will take place. Therefore, although the Old Testament does not speak of the "second coming of Christ" or of His return *in these very words,* it predicts that He will come in a certain manner and for a specific ministry to mankind in which He has not yet come. This must, then, be a coming of Christ which is yet future. Since He has come *once* in another way, He must come *again* in fulfilment of these prophecies of God's unfailing Word. In this sense, therefore the Old Testament predicts Christ's second advent, His coming to the earth to set up His kingdom over Israel and the nations.

2. The Witness of the New Testament to the Return of Christ

One can scarcely read the New Testament without discovering in a short time that it declares again and again that the Lord Jesus Christ will return. He Himself thus promised, while He was still on the earth: "I will come again" (John 14:3); "Immediately after the tribulation of those days shall the sun be darkened . . . and then shall appear the sign of the Son of man in heaven: and then shall all the tribes of the earth mourn, and they shall see the Son of man coming in the clouds of heaven with power and great glory" (Matt. 24:29, 30); "When the Son of man shall come in His glory, and all the holy angels with Him, then shall He sit upon the throne of His glory" (Matt. 25:31). From heaven itself our Lord made the same promise, through the Apostle John, His last recorded words in Holy Writ: "Surely I come quickly" (Rev. 22:20).

The angels testified, when our Lord ascended from the earth into heaven, that He will come again: "Ye men of Galilee, why stand ye gazing up into heaven? This same Jesus . . . shall so come in like manner as ye have seen Him go into heaven" (Acts 1:11).

The Apostle Paul taught Christ's return: "When Christ, who is our life, shall appear, then shall ye also appear with Him in glory" (Col. 3:4); ". . . we should live soberly, righteously, and godly, in this present world; looking for that blessed hope, and the glorious appearing of the great God and our Saviour Jesus Christ" (Titus 2:12, 13).

Peter witnessed to Christ's second advent also: "For we have not followed cunningly devised fables, when we made known unto you the power and coming of our Lord Jesus Christ, but were eyewitnesses of His majesty" (II Peter 1:16).

So did John bear testimony to Christ's return: "Beloved, now are we the sons of God, and it doth not yet appear what we shall be: but we know that, when He shall appear, we shall be like Him, for we shall see Him as He is" (I John 3:2).

Either the Lord Jesus Christ made these promises about His return, or He did not. Either the angels and apostles declared He would come again, or they did not. If our Lord and the penmen of the New Testament did not so testify, then the Bible is not true. If they did so prophesy, and if the Scriptures are inspired of the Holy Spirit, then Christ is coming again.

3. The Nature and Manner of Christ's Return

The coming of the Lord, as it is told by Christ Himself, and by angels, prophets, and apostles, and as it is written in God's Word, is neither the spirit of Christ permeating the world nor the gift of the Holy Spirit. In the case of the former, while it is perfectly true that believers in the Lord Jesus Christ are called "the salt of the earth" and "the light of the world" (Matt. 5:12, 13), they cannot be said, by any stretch of the imagination, to be Christ in His coming, nor is the organized church the Lord resident upon earth. As to the coming of the Holy

Spirit, it is altogether a different thing from Christ's personal return.

The gift of the Spirit is expressed in a terminology that leaves no room for confusing it with the second advent of the Lord. The Holy Spirit's coming was foretold in these words: "It is expedient for you that I go away," our Lord said to His disciples: "for if I go not away, the Comforter will not come unto you: but if I depart, I will send Him unto you. . . . Howbeit, when He, the Spirit of truth, is come, He will guide you into all truth" (John 16:7, 13). *To come oneself* is quite a different thing from *sending someone else*. Furthermore, the Spirit's coming was promised as a gift during Christ's absence. And again, He, the Holy Spirit, has already come (Acts 2:4). He was here on earth when Paul, and Peter, and John spoke of the coming of the Lord as yet future. The Spirit was here when the ascended Christ declared: "Surely I come quickly."

The return of Christ is not the coming of a spirit, an apparition, a phantom. It is the coming of the Lord Himself. He will be seen (Matt. 24:30). His return will not only be visible but it will be a bodily return. He will come in the same body with which He ascended: "This same Jesus, which is taken up from you into heaven, shall so come in like manner as ye have seen Him go" (Acts 1:11). He left visibly; He will return visibly. He ascended in a body; He will descend in a body. He departed from the earth, and He will come again to the earth. It is the Lord *Himself* who will come again (I Thess. 4:16).

4. Christ's Return in Relation to the Millennium

In respect to the return of Christ, there are three schools of interpretation as to the relation of that advent to the Millennium. These viewpoints are known as Amillennialism, Postmillennialism, and Premillennialism.

The word "millennium" is from two Latin words, *mille* and

annus, and means *a thousand years; a* means *without, post* denotes *after,* and *pre* signifies *before.*

The Amillennialists teach that there will be no Millennium,
no "golden age" on earth during which Christ will reign but
that, rather, the promises to Israel of old are fulfilled in the
Church today. The Amillennialists hold that Christ will come
again in judgment; that the righteous dead and wicked dead
will both be raised at that time; and that, following the judgment, there will be the new heavens and new earth.

The Postmillennialists believe and teach that there will be a
Millennium; that it will be ushered in by the efforts of the
Church, as it were; and that it will not be until after the
Millennium that Christ will come, when He will reward His
own, judge His enemies, and establish the new heavens and
new earth.

The chief differences between the Amillennialists and Postmillennialists lie in (1) the fact of a Millennium; and (2) that,
while the former may look for the coming of Christ in their
own lifetime, or for signs of His coming, the latter cannot expect him for at least a thousand years, unless the Millennium
has already begun.

The Premillennialists hold that it will be the coming of
Christ that will bring about the Millennium; that He will
reign over the earth from the throne of His father, David, for
a thousand years; and that there is a period of that length
between the resurrection of the just and the resurrection of the
wicked dead for judgment.

The amillennial and postmillennial interpretations cannot
by any means be dismissed with a wave of the hand. Nevertheless, because the purpose of this study has not to do with
these views primarily but with the premillennial interpretation,
we must simply state our own estimates of Amillennialism and
Postmillennialism in an exceedingly brief way, reserving exam-
inations of certain of their proposals until the proper place.

We are convinced that Amillennialism errs grievously in disregarding the promises to Israel concerning an earthly kingdom, ascribing these promises to the Church. The Church has a heavenly calling and hope, not an earthly prospect. So too, by the way, has every Israelite in this present age who confesses Jesus Christ as the Messiah of God, and trusts in Him as Lord and Saviour. Neither do we believe that the "thousand years," mentioned six times in Revelation 20, can be ignored, in spite of the fact that the Apocalypse is a symbolic book. According to this chapter, there is a millennium between the first resurrection and the resurrection of the wicked dead.

Postmillennialism, we affirm, ignores one very clear note in predictive Scripture: that as the age advances in time it deteriorates in character. There is no Scripture to suggest that men can themselves bring in the Millennium, an age of peace and righteous rule, and this holds even for the Church. Things are not to improve during this age, but evil will wax worse and worse, and professing Christianity will apostatize so that, when our Lord comes, the faith will be sparse indeed (II Tim. 3; II Thess. 2; Luke 18:8).

It is our conviction that Amillennialism and Postmillennialism do not teach the true doctrine of the Scriptures but that the premillennial interpretation of prophetic truth is the correct one; and it is with a phase of Premillennialism that this study has to do.

5. The Return of Christ for His Church

That the Lord, when He comes in power and great glory, will be accompanied by myriads of His people is not a fact that was reserved by God for revelation in the New Testament. As far back as the days of Enoch, Christ's return with His people was known: "And Enoch also, the seventh from Adam," Jude tells us, "prophesied of these, saying, Behold, the Lord cometh with ten thousands of His saints" (vs. 14). This fact is amply confirmed in the New Testament, as, for example, in Revelation 19:11–16, where there is recorded the description of the glorious coming of the living Word of God as King of kings and Lord of lords. It stands to reason, therefore, that if Christ is to come with His saints, they must be raised before His coming.

There is a phase of that assembling of the saints with the Saviour that was not disclosed, however, until the Church was born. It was intimated by our Lord when He told His disciples that He would come again and receive them to Himself (John 14:3). But the revelation was made more complete through the Apostle Paul, first to the Thessalonians, to whom he divulged that, when the dead in Christ should be raised, a living generation, on earth at Christ's coming, would be caught up with those raised from the grave (I Thess. 4:15–17); and second to the Corinthians, to whom he made known the mystery: "We shall not all sleep, but we shall all be changed, in a moment, in the twinkling of an eye, at the last trump: for the trumpet shall sound, and the dead shall be raised incorruptible, and we shall be changed. For this corruptible must put on incorruption, and this mortal must put on immortality" (I Cor. 15:51–53).

This translation of a living generation of believers from bodies corruptible to bodies of incorruption and glory, at the coming of the Lord, is what is known as the Rapture of the Church; and it is with this, and its relation in time to the period of tribulation that is to come upon this earth, that these pages will be occupied.

6. The Tribulation—Its Duration and Relation, in Time, to the Millennium

It is important that we understand what the Tribulation is and its place in predictive prophecy.

In the Book of Daniel, chapter 9, we find the prophet

perusing, with his face set toward God in prayer, supplication, and fasting, Jeremiah's prophecy pertaining to the seventy years of Babylonian captivity which Daniel's people were obliged to sufler, during which Jerusalem was in desolation (Jer. 25:11, 12). Daniel identified himself with his people in his prayer, confessing the iniquities of Judah, of the inhabitants of Jerusalem, and of all Israel, and besought the Lord that He might cause His face to shine once again upon His sanctuary, now desolate, and to forgive the sins of His chosen people. While Daniel was praying, and confessing his sins and those of the nation, a messenger of God, the angel Gabriel, confronted him, touching him and informing him that he had been sent to Daniel to give him skill and understanding. Thereupon Gabriel predicted that a period of seventy weeks had been determined concerning Daniel's people, Israel, and the angel outlined what was to take place during that time, generally designated by students of the prophetic Word as "Daniel's Seventy Weeks."

These seventy weeks are not to be understood to mean, of necessity, weeks of seven days. They are, rather, heptads, or periods of seven. They might thus denote spans of seventy times seven days, or years, or decades, or centuries. Daniel could not know which it was, at the time that he heard the prophecy and recorded it. History has revealed, however, that these "weeks" were weeks of years, each being a period of seven years' duration.

It is to be observed that certain things were predicted concerning Israel, Daniel's people, and Jerusalem, the holy city, after which there would be an end of their transgressions, reconciliation for iniquity, the establishment of everlasting righteousness, the conclusion of the prophecy, and the anointing of the Most High. The events that were to precede the fulfilment of the matters delineated in verse 24, as stated above, were: (1) the restoring and building of Jerusalem; (2) the coming and cutting off of Messiah; (3) the destruction of the city of Jerusalem and the temple; (4) a covenant to be made with a coming prince; (5) the breaking of the covenant; (6) the cessation of the sacrifices and the desolation of the altar; and (7) the destruction of the desolate or the desolator.

Gabriel stated that "from the going forth of the commandment to restore and to build Jerusalem unto the Messiah the Prince shall be seven weeks, and three score and two weeks: the street shall be built again, and the wall, even in troublous times" (vs. 25). Here are two periods of heptads—one of seven, and the other of sixty-two—totaling sixty-nine heptads. The commandment to restore and build Jerusalem was given, as the Scripture shows us, by Artaxerxes the king (Artaxerxes Longimanus, the son of Ahasuerus, Esther 1:1), in the month of Nisan (April), in the twentieth year of his reign, that is, 445 B. C. (Neh. 2:1-8).* In the first seven weeks, a period of 49 years, the city and its walls were rebuilt; in the next sixty-two weeks, 434 years, Messiah came and fulfilled His ministry. Thus we know from history that the "weeks" of Daniel's prophecy are periods of seven years each.

"And after threescore and two weeks shall Messiah be cut off, but not for Himself" (vs. 26). Forty-nine years (seven weeks) plus 434 years (sixty-two weeks) equals 483 years; and 483 years after 445 B. C. would be A. D. 38. But prophetic years equal only 360 days each, so that approximately seven years must be subtracted, bringing the date that "Messiah [should be] cut off, but not for Himself," to A. D. 31, the time most generally agreed upon by students of Bible chronology as the year of Christ's crucifixion, which was assuredly not for Himself but for the sins of many (Mark 10:45; II Cor. 5:21; I Pet. 2:24).

---

* The command is not to be confused with that of Cyrus to rebuild the house of the Lord, the temple in Jerusalem (II Chron. 36:23; Ezra 1:3).

Gabriel told Daniel that, subsequently, "the people of the prince that shall come shall destroy the city and the sanctuary" (vs. 26), and this was surely accomplished by Rome under Titus, in A. D. 70. Observe that the prince to come, here mentioned, is not identical with Messiah the Prince. Christ did not destroy the city or the sanctuary, nor will He do so. Neither, as a matter of fact, was it predicted that the coming prince would do this, but his people. It is evident, therefore, that since the destruction was wrought by Rome, the prince to come is a Roman. He is the head of the ten-kingdom power, the revived Roman Empire, spoken of in Revelation 13:1–8.

But only sixty-nine weeks of Daniel's prophecy have been fulfilled. What about the final week? It is yet to come. Presently, as all through this parenthetic age in which we are living, God is not dealing with Israel as a nation. The remnant is not in Jerusalem. We are living now in the times of the Gentiles, and not until a remnant of Israel that believes God's Word and owns His Christ—not all of Israel, mind you, but a remnant—is back in the land and the city, will God let His face shine upon the nation again. Jerusalem has been trodden down of the Gentiles in this intervening period.

The final week of Daniel's prophecy will doubtless be another week of seven years. It is yet to come. Concerning it, Daniel says: "And he [the prince that shall come] shall confirm the covenant with many for one week: and in the midst of the week he shall cause the sacrifice and oblation to cease, and for the overspreading of abominations he shall make it desolate, even until the consummation, and that determined shall be poured upon the desolate" (vs. 27). This is Daniel's Seventieth Week. It has to do in great part with Israel and the land of Palestine. It is the period that we know as "the Tribulation," concerning which the prophet spoke further, in chapter 12:1; about which our Lord prophesied, in that which is known as "the Olivet Discourse" (Matt. 24; 25); and regarding which the greater portion of The Revelation is occupied (chaps. 6–19).

The Tribulation, the Seventieth Week of Daniel's prophecy, is itself divided into two parts, as intimated by the prediction that, "in the midst of the week," the coming prince will break the covenant that he has made with many. Each of these two parts, spoken of in terms such as "a time and times and the dividing of time" (Dan. 7:25), "a time, times, and an half" (Dan. 12:7), "forty and two months" (Rev. 13:5), "a thousand two hundred and threescore days" (Rev. 11:3; 12:6), consists of three and one-half years, or one-half of the Tribulation. The latter half, that is, the last three and one-half years of Daniel's Seventieth Week, is spoken of in the Scriptures as "the time of Jacob's trouble" (Jer. 30:7), and the Great Tribulation (Matt. 24:15–21).

There can be no question as to where the final week of the seventy fits into the prophetic scheme of things. It immediately precedes the Millennium, the kingdom age, for it culminates in the return of Christ in power and great glory, as He Himself predicted: "Immediately *after* the tribulation of those days shall the sun be darkened, and the moon shall not give her light, and the stars shall fall from heaven, and the powers of the heavens shall be shaken: and then shall appear the sign of the Son of man in heaven: and then shall all the tribes of the earth mourn, and they shall see the Son of man coming in the clouds of heaven with power and great glory. . . . When the Son of man shall come in His glory, and all the holy angels with Him, then shall He sit upon the throne of His glory" (Matt. 24:29, 30; 25:31; cf. Rev. 19:11–20:6).

7. Various Viewpoints as to the Time of Rapture in Relation to the Tribulation

There are four viewpoints as to what the Scriptures teach in relation to the time of the translation of the Church in respect to the Tribulation. They may be described in the following terms: (1) Pre-Tribulationism, which maintains that our Lord will come for His own, the dead in Christ and a living generation of believers, before the Tribulation is ushered in; (2) Mid-Tribulationism, whose proponents teach that the translation of the Church will take place halfway through Daniel's Seventieth Week, at the sounding of the seventh trumpet of Revelation; (3) Post-Tribulationism, which sug- *Right one* gests that it will be after the period of Jacob's trouble, at the same general time as Christ returns in power, that He will rapture the Church; and (4) Partial-Rapturism, which holds that only a portion of the Church will be taken up before the Tribulation, those who are looking for Christ's coming, the balance being left until midway through this prophetic week or until its end. We shall discuss each of these four views in our studies, some more than others, examining the Word of God to learn what it has to say on the whole subject. For we must remember that there can only be one true interpretation of any Scripture, although there may be many applications.

8. Heresy Is Not Involved

When we come to our conclusion, or when we examine the Scriptures and discover this view or that one to be contrary to what we believe is proper interpretation, we must be careful not to brand those with whom we disagree heretics, or their doctrine heresy. The Person and work of Christ are not involved in this matter. All who are true believers in Christ, who are, indeed, looking for His coming, are members of one family. All who hold one of the four views enumerated above, as to the time and manner of Christ's coming for His Church in relation to the Tribulation, and who know why they believe as they do, are earnest Christians, and there ought not to be division among us. It is regrettable that this has not always been the case but that, on the contrary, fellowship has been broken between brethren who differ on such matters, and doors of utterance have been closed to gifted and godly saints because they understand some of these predictive Scriptures differently from us. "My brethren, these things ought not so to be." Already there is far too much discord among God's people. Members of the same family should be able to disagree without being disagreeable about it.

Were the Scriptures wholly transparent upon this subject, a detail in the vast program of the last days, there would be no room for varying opinions. But there are points to be considered in all four of the "interpretations" that we have mentioned, and there are beloved servants of the Lord who adhere to each of them. We have never known one child of God among those who have sincerely sought to discover the truth in this matter, who has not been a devoted Christian, an earnest soul-winner, and who has not been seeking, in the Spirit's power, to live close to the Lord and to walk in a godly way.

How tragic it would be if such esteemed and beloved saints, all now with the Lord, as James M. Gray, A. C. Gaebelein, H. A. Ironside, and William L. Pettingill on the one hand; G. H. Pember, J. A. Seiss, D. M. Panton, and J. Hudson Taylor on another; and George Müller, S. P. Tregelles, Dan Crawford, and Henry W. Frost on still another, should have pointed the finger at those in other groups, crying, "Heretic!" and refusing to have fellowship one band with another! Yet the first four of these brethren were pre-tribulationists; the second four, partial-rapturists; and the last four post-tribulationists. They are in the glory now, and in whatsoever way any of them, or all of them, erred, they are now instructed as to the truth, we can be sure. May we, therefore, be kept from bitterness in any remarks that we make, and bear in mind that controversy in itself is not wrong but is an instrument for the guardianship of the truth as opposed to error. Let us endeavor to guard, in it all, "the unity of the Spirit in the bond of peace."

9. Tradition and the Word of God

Tradition does not of necessity warrant the truth of any matter, unless that tradition be soundly rooted in the revelation of God. But neither is tradition to be cast aside merely because it is tradition. The sole arbiter in reaching our conclusion, however, must be the Word of God.

An Old Testament prophet declared: "To the law and to the testimony: if they speak not according to this Word, it is because there is no light in them" (Isa. 8:20). And a New Testament apostle asked: "For what saith the Scripture?" (Rom. 4:3). It is in this attitude of seeking divine truth divinely revealed that we shall pursue our subject, with the help of Him who is our final Guide into all truth, the Holy Spirit (John 16:13).

10. Higher Ground

There is one glorious fact in respect to the return of our Lord Jesus Christ that transcends beyond measure the subject matter of this treatise. It has not to do with His coming in relation to the Church but to His coming in power and glory, to be seen of all, to be vindicated before this world-system that rejected Him, and to be accorded due homage, when every knee shall bow before Him and every tongue confess that He is Lord, to the glory of God. May God help us not to have a selfish view of Christ's coming, to be more interested in whether or not we shall escape the Tribulation than we are in Him, to be more concerned that we should be spared suffering than that He should receive His rightful honor. And may God establish within our hearts the longing to see His Beloved and ours, and to be purified by the hope that we have in Him. The study of prophecy is valueless, it is of the flesh, it is but wood, hay, and stubble unless it is motivated by the holy desire for the consummation of all that will redound to the glory of the Lord, and unless it issues in holy living and faithful witness.

CHAPTER II

THE RAPTURE CANNOT BE SEPARATED
FROM RESURRECTION

It was a peculiar mark of the Sadducees that they did not believe in the resurrection of the dead (Mark **12**:18; Luke **20**:27; Acts **23**:8). The members of this sect considered themselves within the fold of Israel but they did not discern the clear revelation of the Scriptures and they denied the might of the Almighty God to raise the dead. No less are there those in our day, who think and speak of themselves as Christians and whose names may be written on the rolls of one church organization or another, who, like the Sadducees, "say there is no resurrection." Of such men we can only state, upon the authority of our Lord Jesus Christ, that they do "err, because [they] know not the Scriptures, neither the power of God" (Mark **12**:24). True Christians accept the Word of God for what it must be, His infallible revelation, and they therefore believe in the resurrection of the dead.

It is very apparent that the translation of the Church is connected with resurrection. There are three New Testament texts that few students of the Bible will deny as being descriptive of the Rapture, namely: I Corinthians **15**:51, 52; I Thessalonians **4**:15–17; and II Thessalonians **2**:1.* Of these

---

* We were about to mention four passages, John **14**:3 being the other text. But we have omitted it with purpose, for two reasons: (1) we have recently learned that there are some Bible students who are convinced that this promise of our Lord's has not to do with the translation of the Church but to Christ's receiving His own to Himself upon their death during all these centuries of the Christian era (an opinion with which we do not agree); and (2), while the promise of John **14**:3 is the first New Testament intimation of the Rapture, it cannot be said to be descriptive of it.

passages, two, the first and the second, declare very clearly *this is right*
that the up-calling of a living generation of believers in Christ
and the resurrection of the dead in Christ are simultaneous.
"Behold, I show you a mystery: We shall not all sleep, but we
shall all be changed, in a moment, in the twinkling of an eye,
at the last trump: for the trumpet shall sound, and the dead
shall be raised incorruptible, and we shall be changed"
(I Cor. 15:51, 52). "But I would not have you to be ignorant,
brethren, concerning them which are asleep . . . For this we say
unto you by the Word of the Lord, that we which are alive
and remain unto the coming of the Lord shall not prevent [pre-
cede] them which are asleep. For the Lord Himself shall descend from heaven with a shout . . . and the dead in Christ shall
rise first: then we which are alive and remain shall be caught
up together with them . . . to meet the Lord in the air . . ."
(I Thess. 4:13, 15–17). It is evident and incontrovertible,
therefore, that the two miraculous events—the resurrection of
those who have died in faith, and the transformation and
translation of those Christians who are living when the rap-
ture-trump of God sounds—will take place simultaneously
and that both groups will be caught up together into Christ's
presence. "At the last trump . . . the dead shall be raised incorruptible, and we shall be changed." "The dead in Christ
shall rise first: then we which are alive and remain shall
be caught up together with them." If, therefore, the time of the
resurrection can be established, as it relates to events of the
last days of this age, then the time of the translation of the
Church, the Rapture, can be settled also.

The Scriptures have a great deal to say about resurrection,
not only in the New Testament but in the Old as well,
although the word "resurrection" is not found in the latter.
Two Old Testament citations, without any effort at exposi-
tion, will suffice to prove the point: (1) "Thy dead men shall
live, together with my dead body shall they arise. Awake

and sing, ye that dwell in dust: for thy dew is as the dew
of herbs, and the earth shall cast out the dead" (Isa. 26:19);
and (2) "And many of them that sleep in the dust of the
earth, shall awake, some to everlasting life, and some to shame
and everlasting contempt" (Dan. 12:2).

As to the New Testament, passages already cited declare
that there will be a resurrection. In Luke 14:14 we read
these words spoken by our Lord: "For thou shalt be recompensed at the resurrection of the just." In John 5:28, 29,
it is recorded that the Lord Jesus said: "Marvel not at this:
for the hour is coming, in the which all that are in the
graves shall hear His voice [the voice of the Son of man, our
Lord Himself], and shall come forth; they that have done
good, unto the resurrection of life; and they that have done
evil, unto the resurrection of damnation." And thrice in John
6, in verses 40, 44, and 54, we find this expression from His
lips: "And I will raise him up at the last day."

The resurrection is taught in the Scriptures; in fact, it is
plain from some of the texts quoted that there are two resurrections spoken of: (1) the resurrection of the just, that will
issue in life; and (2) the resurrection of those who are evil,
that will result in judgment. It is the resurrection of the just
that we are particularly interested in at this time since, quite
obviously, it is not those who have died in their sins but those
who have been justified by faith, the dead "in Christ," who
will be raised and caught up with living believers when the
rapture-shout is sounded.

In each of the Old Testament passages quoted, the context
suggests that the resurrection alluded to will take place in connection with a period of tribulation (Isa. 26:16–18; Dan.
12:1). Bear in mind, however, that these prophecies have particularly to do with Israel and not with the Gentile nations.
The Church, as such, is not involved in these predictions.

In the New Testament Scriptures cited, we observe that the

resurrection of the justified will be "at the last day" (John 6:40, etc.). "The last day"* will be, we assume, the last day of this age, before the new kingdom age is ushered in. As we turn to the book of The Revelation, through the eyes of John we see, after Christ's return in power to destroy His enemies and at the time when the Millennium is to begin, "thrones, and they that sat upon them: and . . . the souls of them that were beheaded for the witness of Jesus, and for the Word of God, and which had not worshipped the beast, neither his image, neither had received his mark upon their foreheads, or in their hands: and they lived and reigned with Christ a thousand years" (20:4). And then we read: "But the rest of the dead lived not again until the thousand years were finished. This is the first resurrection" (vs. 5). Here we have a reference to a resurrection of just men, saints of God, at the last day, after the Tribulation, at the beginning of the Millennium, and it is said to be "the first resurrection." In view of the fact that the translation of the Church is to be identical in time with the resurrection of the just, and on account of the fact that this resurrection, after the Tribulation, is clearly declared to be "the first resurrection," is it not the part of honorable and sane interpretation of Scripture to conclude that the Rapture must be at the same time, that is, after the Tribulation? Indeed it is, *unless* there be other Scriptures which indicate that this cannot be so.

There are other Scriptures which suggest another conclusion, however. But Scripture does not contradict Scripture. It is necessary, therefore, if it is to be understood or proved that the Rapture may occur at another time than that indicated by the first resurrection of Revelation 20, to show that

---

* We must assume that the word "day," as used here, does not necessarily refer to a period of 24 hours but rather to a measure of time, hours or years in duration, during which God will act in a specific manner. For further discussion of this subject, see Chapter IX, page 82.

the first resurrection does not consist of one united up-calling of all who have died in faith but, rather, a series of such resurrections.

Not for an instant do we suggest that Scripture can be added to. The Bible speaks of two resurrections: the resurrection of the just, and the resurrection of the wicked dead. There are not three or four resurrections; there are two, and no more. We should immediately place them as occurring at two distinct times—the first, as written in Revelation 20:4; and the second, which issues in the second death, at the time indicated in verses 11–15, were it not that there are other Scriptures which lead us to investigate further. The important thing to discover is whether or not the first resurrection must be a simultaneous resurrection of all the just at one definite moment, or whether the first resurrection may be understood to mean the resurrection of all the just, to be sure, but in a series of two or more ascensions.

It is quickly apparent that there is not the slightest suggestion, in all the predictions concerning the resurrection of the just, that that resurrection will do anything other than take place at one time. But it is equally clear that, in respect to the resurrection of the just and that of wicked dead, it might easily be understood, at first reading, that these two resurrections will occur simultaneously. For example, here are the words of our Lord, already cited once: ". . . the hour is coming, in the which all that are in the graves shall hear His voice, and shall come forth; they that have done good, unto the resurrection of life, and they that have done evil, unto the resurrection of damnation" (John 5:28, 29; cf. Dan. 12:2). "*The hour* is coming," our Lord said, in which all in the graves are to be raised, some to life and some to judgment. Who would suppose, in reading this language, that there is to be an interval of a thousand years between the two resurrections of this "hour"? Yet, when we get to Revelation 20, we find that this is so.

said, in connection with the
'this is the second death." If
›wed in our interpretation of
important to insist that the
ath," embraces all those, with-
he eternal judgment in the lake
-15, as it is to state categorically
s the first resurrection," includes
who will be raised to life and will
sand years. Yet in the case of the
e who will be consigned to its judg-
nousand years before the judgment
e, namely, the beast and the false
'he second death, then, falls upon
ct occasions, separated by a thousand
years. ___ the false prophet, the condemnation
that they will rec___ as surely "the second death" as it will
be for those brought before the great white throne.

It is therefore wholly conceivable that "the first resurrection" will be experienced, by those who have been justified
by God, in certain distinctly separate periods, perhaps three
and one-half years apart, perhaps seven, perhaps more. Christ
Himself is the "firstfruits of them that slept" (I Cor. **25**:20).
The firstfruits are the earliest (Heb., *bikkur*) and chief (Heb.,
reshith) fruits of the harvest, yet it is all one harvest. The question arises, too, as to whether the resurrection of the two witness of Revelation **11**:1-12 does not precede that spoken of in
chapter **20**:4-6. Yet who will deny that the two witnesses are
partakers of that which is called "the first resurrection"? Those
who will be raised are of the same resurrection as the Lord
Jesus—the first resurrection. "But every man in his own order:
Christ the firstfruits; afterward they that are Christ's at His
coming" (I Cor. **15**:23). All of these, excepting Christ Himself, who will share in the first resurrection will do so "at His
coming." It remains to be seen what is involved in that coming.

CHAPTER III

DISTINGUISHING THINGS THAT DIFFER

In the study of the Bible it is important to correlate things that agree but it is equally essential to distinguish between things that differ. "Precept must be upon precept, precept upon precept; line upon line, line upon line; here a little, and there a little" (Isa. 28:10). This is the order of instruction which will enable the most immature believer to obtain knowledge and understand doctrine. However, we must also learn in our study rightly to divide the Word of truth (II Tim. 2:15). No one can possibly have a clear perception of Scripture as a whole, or of Bible prophecy in particular, who does not discern the distinction between two of the things that differ, namely, Israel and the Church.

One or two illustrations will serve to clarify this point. The Psalmist could sing with perfect propriety: "O daughter of Babylon, who art to be destroyed; happy shall he be, that rewardeth thee as thou hast served us. Happy shall he be, that taketh and dasheth thy little ones against the stones" (Psa. 137:8, 9). Such language, however, would be out of place and contrary to the mind of God in the mouth of a Christian; for we are told: "Dearly beloved, avenge not yourselves, but rather give place unto wrath: for it is written, Vengeance is Mine . . . saith the Lord. Therefore if thine enemy hunger, feed him; if he thirst, give him drink: for in so doing thou shalt heap coals of fire on his head" (Rom. 12:19, 20).

In the former case, we have the utterance of an Israelite who had been placed under the divine law which declared: "Eye for eye, tooth for tooth, hand for hand, foot for foot, burning for burning, wound for wound, stripe for stripe" (Ex. 21:24, 25). This was right and proper in its season, but He who made the law was privileged to repeal it, and this He did in the new economy. For God the Son taught His followers, who were the initial converts to Himself and the earliest proponents of the Gospel of grace: "Ye have heard that it hath been said, An eye for an eye, and a tooth for a tooth: but I say unto you, That ye resist not evil; but whosoever shall smite thee on thy right cheek, turn to him the other also" (Matt. 5:38, 39). When our Lord Himself was reviled, He reviled not again; and the Apostle Paul, when he was smitten by the high priest, Ananias, did not return the blow but committed the matter to God. The proper behavior for the Christian is written in Ephesians 5:1, 2: "Be ye therefore followers of God, as dear children: and walk in love, as Christ also hath loved us, and hath given Himself for us an offering and a sacrifice to God for a sweet smelling savour."

In Ecclesiastes it is said: "To every thing there is a season, and a time to every purpose under the heaven . . . He [God] hath made every thing beautiful in His time" (3:1, 11). If the truths of God's Word are withdrawn from their season and dissociated from their pertinent time, however, their harmony is disturbed and their teaching obscured.

There is a marked difference in the Scriptures between Israel and the Church in respect to their calling. Israel's calling was earthly while the Church's calling is heavenly. This does not mean that Israelites were not the beneficiaries of spiritual blessings, nor does it suggest that they were not, by faith in the coming Redeemer to whom the blood sacrifices of the Mosaic economy pointed, the recipients of everlasting salvation. Moreover, it is not an intimation that no individual Christian has received, by God's grace, earthly riches and honor. It is however, a statement that corporately, as a body, Israel's portion, under the promises of God, is on earth (Gen. 12:1-3; 13:14, 15; 15:18; 17:8; Deut. 11:12; etc.), whereas the Church, as a body, is blessed "with all spiritual blessings in heavenly places in Christ" (Eph. 1:3), and the members

of this body become together "partakers of the heavenly calling" (Heb. 3:1).

Other variances between the divine program for Israel and
the Church are manifold. To Israel greatness, wealth, and
honor were promised in token of God's favor upon His people.
"Praise ye the Lord. Blessed is the man that feareth the Lord,
that delighteth greatly in His commandments. His seed shall be
mighty upon the earth. . . . Wealth and riches shall be in his
house: and his righteousness endureth for ever" (Psa. 112:1–3;
see also Gen. 12:2; Deut. 28:12, 13; II Sam. 5:19; II Chron.
1:12; etc.). Where can any such promise be found for the
Church? On the contrary, "not many wise men after the flesh,
not many mighty, not many noble, are called: but God hath
chosen the foolish things of the world to confound the wise . . .
and base things of the world, and things which are despised,
hath God chosen, yea, and things which are not, to bring to
nought things that are: that no flesh should glory in His presence" (I Cor. 1:26–29). Our Lord said to His followers, on the
night of His betrayal: "If the world hate you, ye know that it
hated Me before it hated you. If ye were of the world, the
world would love its own: but because ye are not of the world,
but I have chosen you out of the world, therefore the world
hateth you" (John 15:18, 19); and again: "In the world ye
shall have tribulation" (John 16:33). And the Apostle Paul
declared: "Yea, and all that will live godly in Christ Jesus
shall suffer persecution" (II Tim. 3:12).

Still another distinction between Israel and the Church is
the mode of worship. Under the old economy, approach to
God was through a specified priesthood, continued in succes-
sion in a particular family. Early a tabernacle was erected in
the wilderness, and later the temple was built in Jerusalem.
Here God must be worshipped, in "the place which the Lord
thy God shall choose to place His name there" (Deut. 26:2).
The ministry of the Levitical priesthood, the offerings of the

people and priests, the holy place, and the Holy of holies are well known to students of the Bible. Specific regulations governed every approach to Jehovah. He was accessible only on a certain day and by means of certain ordinances, and then only to the high priest. But when the Son of God was made flesh, when His work of redemption was accomplished at Calvary, He cried: "It is finished!" The veil of the temple was rent in twain from top to bottom. And now, in this Church age, every believer in the Lord Jesus Christ, Jew or Gentile, bond or free, illiterate or highly educated, mature Christian or babe in Christ, can with perfect propriety have "boldness to enter into the Holiest by the blood of Jesus, by a new and living way, which He hath consecrated for us, through the veil, that is to say, His flesh; and, having an High Priest over the house of God . . . draw near with a true heart in full assurance of faith" (Heb. 10:19–22).

The differentiation between the calling of Israel and the Church, so evident in the few Scriptures that have been cited, is equally manifest in predictive prophecy. While it is quite true that, in this present economy, there is no difference between the believing Jew and the believing Gentile, but that all believers have been made one in Christ (Gal. 3:7, 28, 29), this fact in no way annuls the promises that God made to Israel as a nation and which have not to this time been fulfilled. The difficulty is not to find Scriptures to establish the matter but to select citations from among the multitude of such predictions that exist.

Very early in Israel's history prophecies were made concerning their literal banishment from the land that God gave them and, at the same time, equally clear promises were given as to their literal restoration to the land, predictions that are absolute, depending not upon the faithfulness of Israel but upon the faithfulness of Jehovah to keep His covenant. The subsequent faithfulness of the nation will flow from the empower-

ment of the sovereign grace of God exactly as any exercise of
faithfulness on the part of members of the Church today issues
from His power and grace.

As far back as Leviticus, there is a prophecy that very evidently reaches forward to the time of the destruction of Jerusalem by Titus, and we read: "The land also shall be left of
them [Israel], and shall enjoy her sabbaths, while she lieth
desolate without them: and they shall accept of the punishment of their iniquity: because, even because they despised My
judgments, and because their soul abhorred My statutes. And
yet for all that, when they be in the land of their enemies, I
will not cast them away, neither will I abhor them, to destroy
them utterly, and to break My covenant with them: for I am
the Lord their God. But I will for their sakes remember the
covenant of their ancestors, whom I brought forth out of the
land of Egypt in the sight of the heathen, that I might be their
God: I am the Lord. These are the statutes and judgments
and laws, which the Lord made between Him and the children
of Israel in mount Sinai by the hand of Moses" (Lev. 26:43–
46).

Again, just prior to Israel's entrance into the land of
promise, Jehovah pledged them: "And it shall come to pass,
when all these things are come upon thee, the blessing and the
curse, which I have set before thee, and thou shalt call them
to mind among all the nations, whither the Lord thy God hath
driven thee, and shalt return unto the Lord thy God, and shalt
obey His voice according to all that I command thee this day,
thou and thy children, with all thine heart, and with all thy
soul; that then the Lord thy God will turn thy captivity, and
have compassion upon thee, and will return and gather thee
from the nations, whither the Lord thy God hath scattered
thee. If any of thine be driven out unto the outmost parts of
heaven, from thence will the Lord thy God gather thee,
and from thence will He fetch thee: and the Lord thy God

will bring thee into the land which thy fathers possessed, and thou shalt possess it; and He will do thee good, and multiply thee above thy fathers. And the Lord thy God will circumcise thine heart, and the heart of thy seed, to love the Lord thy God with all thine heart, and with all thy soul, that thou mayest live" (Deut. 30:1–6). No such thing has been fulfilled to this time.

We might cite in turn prophecies in the Psalms, in Isaiah, and in Ezekiel; we might search them out in Daniel, Hosea, Joel, Amos, Obadiah, Micah, Nahum, Zephaniah, Haggai, Zecharaiah, and Malachi, for they are there. But we shall conclude these quotations with a familiar word from Jeremiah: "Therefore, behold, the days come, saith the Lord, that they shall no more say, The Lord liveth, which brought up the children of Israel out of the land of Egypt; but, The Lord liveth, which brought up and which led the seed of the house of Israel out of the north country, and from all countries whither I had driven them; and they shall dwell in their own land" (Jer. 23:7, 8).

All of these predictions have to do with an earthly people to be restored to an earthly possession. They have not to do with the Church, whose calling is heavenly and not earthly. How can such Scriptures be applied to the Church, whose members are called from every nation over the face of the earth? The Church has no promised land on earth; the Church has not been driven out of its native habitat to the four corners of the world. The Church is not promised an earthly heritage, but "an inheritance incorruptible, and undefiled, and that fadeth not away, reserved in heaven" (I Pet. 1:4).

When will this restoration of Israel take place? It will be "in the last days," in "the day of the Lord," when He comes to destroy His enemies and to establish righteousness and peace in Jerusalem, a time of blessedness that we speak of as the Millennium (Isa. 2:12; Dan. 2:28; Joel 2; Mic. 4:1, 2).

The distinction between the prophecies that pertain to Israel and those that have to do with the Church must be borne in mind, then, as we examine the time of the Rapture in relation to the Tribulation. Thus, when we turn to the New Testament and find there predictions about the coming of the Lord, and events connected with that advent, we must not read the passages cursorily but examine them and related Scriptures carefully, pursuing our study of them patiently and thoroughly. We must ask ourselves certain questions and discover the answers to them before we arrive at a conclusion, questions such as these: By whom was this word spoken, and to whom? What was the occasion for it? To whom does it relate? What is the general tenor of the Scriptures on this subject?

Here, for example, are two prophecies that relate to the second coming of Christ: Matthew 24:29–31; and I Thessalonians 4:13–18. There are certain similarities about them: both refer to the coming of the Lord, both speak of the sounding of a trumpet, and both suggest a gathering of the Lord's chosen. But there are also notable differences in the two passages: one speaks of cataclysmic signs in the heavens, while the other does not mention them; one Scripture records that the Lord will send His angels "with a great sound of a trumpet," while the other account tells us that it is "the trump of God"; one speaks of the angels gathering the elect, while the other intimates that it is the Lord who will draw them to Himself; in one instance there is no reference to resurrection, while in the other it is stated that "the dead in Christ shall rise."

Do these two passages refer to the same event and to simultaneous developments of that event? Or do these prophecies relate to different phenomena, and is there a time-period between their fulfilments? It is only by ascertaining the proper interpretation of these and kindred passages that we can discover whether the Church will be translated before, during, or after the Tribulation.

CHAPTER IV

IMMEDIATELY AFTER THE TRIBULATION

The classic text that pertains to the translation of the Church is, as almost all will agree. I Thessalonians 4:15–17, for therein more detail is given about the united up-calling of the dead in Christ and a living generation of believers in Him than anywhere else in the Scriptures. We cite the passage, therefore, so as to refresh our minds: "For this we say unto you by the word of the Lord," writes Paul, "that we which are alive and remain unto the coming of the Lord shall not precede* them which are asleep. For the Lord Himself shall descend from heaven with a shout, with the voice of the archangel, and with the trump of God: and the dead in Christ shall rise first: then we which are alive and remain shall be caught up together with them in the clouds, to meet the Lord in the air: and so shall we ever be with the Lord."

It is argued, by those who teach that the Church will pass through the Tribulation, that the phenomenon described in I Thessalonians 4 is identical with certain other events predicted in the New Testament, as, for example, that which is recorded in Matthew 24:29–31, etc. "This [Matthew 24:29–31] is the rapture," they say; and it is suggested that those who do not acquiesce in this opinion are guilty of insinuating that Christ and Paul do not agree. It is further submitted that, to understand and teach the Matthew passage as alluding to a different event from the Thessalonian account, is to "make dark, what is clear; complicated, what is simplicity itself; and

* We have used the word, "precede," in this citation, rather than the archaic "prevent" of the Authorized Version, to clarify the sense of the passage.

contradictory, what is beautifully harmonious." This the pre-tribulationists do, it is said, in order to "escape" the Tribulation. God forbid that we should "make" the Scriptures say anything, or that we should imagine that we can, by interpretation, escape aught that God has prescribed for us. Suppose we examine Matthew 24 in some detail and ascertain whether verses 29–31 relate to that which is set forth in I Thessalonians 4:15–17.

There is no question as to the time, in relation to the Tribulation, of the coming of the Lord announced in Matthew 24:29–31: it is *"immediately after* the tribulation of those days" (vs. 29). The whole chapter, a portion of that which is known as our Lord's Olivet Discourse, relates to the subject of the Tribulation.

With this Scripture, as with other Scriptures, it is well to discover by whom the message is spoken, to whom, and the entire purport of it. The discourse is introduced through a question that our Lord's disciples asked Him, or rather, several questions, namely: "When shall these things be? And what shall be the sign of Thy coming, and of the end of the world," that is, literally, "the consummation of the age?" (vs. 3).

The first question came from the disciples in response to Christ's statement concerning the temple in Jerusalem: "See ye not all these things? Verily I say unto you, There shall not be left here one stone upon another, that shall not be thrown down." It is quite generally recognized that in this prediction, as with certain other prophecies of the Bible, there were two occasions in the mind of the Lord—the near view, and the far view. As an illustration of this, observe the covenant that God made with David, written in II Samuel 7:4–16. In the near view, and in part, this promise was fulfilled in Solomon, but the far view comprehended David's greater Son, our Lord Jesus Christ, and the prophecy was never completely accomplished in Solomon. So here in Matthew 24, the disciples' first question, "When shall these things be?" was answered in a way that foretold the destruction of Jerusalem and the temple in A. D. 70 by Titus; but the answer looked beyond that occasion, embodying with it the answer to the other part of the question, as to the signs that would appear in connection with the coming of the Lord and the end of the age.

The disciples knew nothing about the translation of the Church, a mystery revealed to Paul a quarter of a century later and, by him, to the Church (I Thess. 4:13ff; I Cor. 15: 51ff) which was, until that time, ignorant of it. What the disciples were interested in, on the occasion of the Olivet interrogations, was something about which they had at least a smattering of knowledge—the coming of the Lord to establish His earthly kingdom. Their query was in the same spirit and of the same essence as one that they made later, when our Lord was about to depart from them: "Lord, wilt Thou at this time restore again the kingdom to Israel?" (Acts 1:6). And it is quite evident that Christ's reply pertained to that which had been asked of Him.

It has already been observed that the introductory words of verse 29, "immediately after the tribulation of those days," identify the time-period of the fulfilment of this prophecy. That it is the Tribulation is abundantly substantiated, in verses 4–28, by the following facts: (1) the order and nature of the trials to come during this time, which are more than incidentally similar to the breaking of the seals, in Revelation 6, where the Tribulation is introduced in that book of prophecy; (2) the reference to "the abomination of desolation, spoken of by Daniel the prophet," a prophecy that has to do with Daniel's Seventieth Week, that is, the Tribulation (Dan. 9:27; 11:31; 12:11); and (3) the specific mention, in verse 21, that "then shall be great tribulation, such as was not since the beginning of the world to this time, no, nor ever shall be."

It is important to note, as delinated in the Olivet Discourse, the character and activity of those who are to live during this period of tribulation, and God's dealings with them. The scene is in Jerusalem, where the temple will be, and in Judaea. The law of the sabbath appears to prevail, a condition that is distinctly Jewish. The Gospel of the kingdom is the message that is to be preached. This does not sound as if it applies to the Church. The Church is composed of believers out of all nations and localities. The Jerusalem temple has no place in the Church's program. The Church worships on the first day of the week and is not bound by such Levitical restrictions as a sabbath day's journey. The Gospel that we proclaim is known throughout the epistles, where Church truth is most fully revealed, as the Gospel of God, the Gospel of Christ, the Gospel of our Lord Jesus Christ, our Gospel, etc., and is never spoken of therein as the Gospel of the kingdom.*

From the very beginning to the end, the Olivet Discourse has a Jewish cast. It is true that the disciples, who heard this message from the Mount of Olives, were at the same time both Jews and members of the Church; for while the Church was not yet founded when this prophecy was made, Christ knew that those seated before Him, His followers whom He had taught, would be born into the Church on the day of Pentecost and would thus constitute the earliest members of His mystical body. Since in His foreknowledge it was perfectly evident to our Lord that none of these men would be living,

---

* The Gospel of the kingdom, the Gospel of grace, the Gospel of God, the Gospel of Christ, etc., are all connected with the kingdom of God. Our Lord spoke of things that pertained to the kingdom of God (Acts 1:3); and Paul preached the kingdom of God (Acts 20:25) and taught it (Rom. 14:17; I Cor. 6:9, 10; Col. 4:11). But the *Gospel* of the kingdom that our Lord preached when He first presented Himself to His people, Israel (Matt. 4:23), is the Gospel that the forerunner, John the Baptist, announced and that He Himself proclaimed: "Repent ye: for the kingdom of heaven (or, *the heavens*) is at hand" (Matt. 3:2; 4:17). This, surely, is the Gospel referred to in the Olivet Discourse: "This Gospel of the kingdom shall be preached in all the world unto all nations; and then shall the end come" (Matt. 24:14).

either at the time of the translation of the Church or when He should return to establish His kingdom on earth, we can be certain that He spoke to them thus, using the pronouns "you" and "ye" as being a representative group. Did they represent Jewish believers in Him, in a Jewish age, the Tribulation? Did they represent the Church at the end of this age? Or were they representative of both groups? It appears extremely unlikely that the Church is suggested here in any way at all, for the very reasons set forth above—that is, the wholly different characteristics, both of the activities and the conditions that will then prevail, from what we understand concerning the Church and the Church age.

When we examine verses 29–31, descriptive of the signs and exercises that will attend the coming of the Son of man, we observe certain things: (1) there will be signs of a phenomenal and cataclysmic nature; (2) Christ will be seen coming by those on the earth, the tribes of the earth mourning; (3) His angels will sound a trumpet; and (4) Christ's angels will gather His elect from the four winds.

Comparing this description with that given of Christ's coming at the time of the Rapture (I Thess. 4:15–17), we note two similarities: (1) the sounding of a trumpet; and (2) the gathering together of the Lord's people. But there are dissimilarities also: (1) in one instance, it appears to be the angels who sound the trumpet, while in the other it is the trump of God; (2) in Matthew, there are said to be amazing signs connected with the coming of the Son of man, whereas in Thessalonians, no signs are mentioned; (3) the gathering of the elect of Matthew 24 is "from the four winds, from one end of heaven to the other," while the gathering of I Thessalonians 4 is a bringing together of dead and living persons, to be caught up into the air to meet the Lord; and (4) there is no resurrection in Matthew 24.

We are ready to acknowledge immediately that, when the

Son of man sends His angels "with a great sound of a trumpet," that trumpet may quite conceivably be "the trump of God." But the remaining dissimilarities between the two prophecies are not as easy to reconcile.

If Matthew 24 speaks of the Rapture, where, in I Thessalonians 4, are the supernatural heavenly movements and sign of the Son of man?

The gathering together of Christ's elect of Matthew 24, designated as "from the four winds, from one end of heaven to the other," is a gathering on earth of God's chosen people, Israel, from the four corners of the earth, whence they have been driven. This is not conjecture. We are prone to think of the elect, in this present age, as the Church, "elect according to the foreknowledge of God" (I Pet. 1:2; Col. 3:12). But Israel was God's elect—"elect" simply means "chosen"—before the Church was formed or even foretold. Thus, for example, we read in the Old Testament: "For Jacob, My servant's sake, and Israel Mine elect" (Isa. 45:4); and again, concerning the seed of Jacob and Judah, that is, Israel the nation: "Mine elect shall inherit it, and My servants shall dwell there" (Isa. 65:9). The rather poetic expression, "the four winds," denotes the four quarters of the earth, and "from one end of heaven to the other" suggests simply this: beneath the vault made by the skies. This gathering is not into the air, as it is in I Thessalonians 4, but it is a gathering of God's elect from all over the earth, back into the land of promise. It is the return to Palestine predicted again and again of old, the occasion when Israel will be restored to Judaea and Jerusalem. It is the fulfilment of an earthly promise to an earthly people, and is not a glorious union of a heavenly people with Christ. How wonderfully it agrees with the promise written in Deuteronomy, for example: "And it shall come to pass, when all these things are come upon thee . . . and thou shalt call them to mind among all the nations, whither the Lord thy God hath driven thee, and shalt return unto the Lord thy God, and shalt obey His voice according to all that I command thee this day, thou and thy children, with all thine heart, and with all thy soul; that then the Lord thy God will turn thy captivity, and have compassion upon thee, and will return and gather thee from all the nations, whither the Lord thy God hath scattered thee. If any of thine be driven out unto the outmost parts of heaven, from thence will the Lord thy God gather thee, and from thence will He fetch thee: and the Lord thy God will bring thee into the land which thy fathers possessed, and thou shalt possess it: and He will do thee good, and multiply thee above thy fathers. And the Lord thy God will circumcise thine heart, and the heart of thy seed, to love the Lord thy God with all thine heart, and with all thy soul, that thou mayest live" (Deut. 30:1–6).

Why, if Matthew 24 speaks of the translation of the Church, is there no mention of resurrection? It has been pointed out, in an earlier chapter, that where the Rapture is there also is resurrection. If the dead are to be raised at the coming of the Son of man, spoken of in Matthew 24, surely such a thing would have been mentioned by our Lord on this occasion.

To state categorically, as some have done in speaking of Matthew 24:29–31, that "this is the Rapture," is not, in our opinion, good exegesis. On the contrary, it would seem to be much more scriptural to state, concerning these verses: "This is *not* the rapture of the Church."

CHAPTER V

FURTHER PROPHECIES IN THE OLIVET DISCOURSE

In addition to our Lord's prediction concerning His coming, recorded in Matthew 24:29–31 and discussed in our last chapter, twice more in the Olivet Discourse He alluded directly to the coming of the Son of man, namely, in chapters 24:37–44 and 25:31–46.

In the former instance He related the conditions that will exist, at the time of His coming, to the days of Noah: "But as the days of Noe were, so shall also the coming of the Son of man be. For as in the days that were before the flood they were eating and drinking, marrying and giving in marriage, until the day that Noe entered into the ark, and knew not until the flood came, and took them all away; so shall also the coming of the Son of man be. Then shall two be in the field; the one shall be taken, and the other left . . . Watch therefore: for ye know not what hour your Lord doth come" (Matt. 24:37–42).

The same circumstances that attended the time just prior to the judgment of the flood will prevail before the return of Christ in judgment upon the world. Business will be going on as usual. People will be occupied with the normal duties of life. The prophets of God, His spokesmen, will be given little heed. Then suddenly the Lord will come. This advent is that described in verses 29–31, "immediately after the tribulation of those days." The whole context indicates that it is this occasion that is here set forth.*

---

* It is suggested, by some who believe that the Church will be on earth during the Tribulation, that Noah is a type of God's people being saved, not *out of*, but *through* judgment. But with equal propriety it

Because it is stated here that two will be in the field, or two women will be grinding at the mill, and that one will be taken and the other left at the coming of the Son of man, some have arrived at the conclusion that it is the translation of the Church that is denoted in the taking of the one and the leaving of the other.† Therefore, say they, the Church must be on earth throughout the Tribulation.

Let us bear in mind, however, that the translation of the Church was not revealed by our Lord but that it was left for the Apostle Paul to declare this mystery as a new revelation (I Cor. 15:51, 52; I Thess. 4:13–18). Consequently, those to whom our Lord was speaking (and we ourselves, had we read the Scriptures only as far as Matthew 24 to this time) could not possibly infer that the Lord's reference to the time of Noah had to do with the rapture of the Church. What would they understand? They would remember that, when the flood came, those who were taken were taken into judgment, and those

---

can be said that Enoch, who was translated before the judgment of the flood (Gen. 5:24; Heb. 11:5) is a type of the Church. Noah's ark certainly gives a picture of Christ saving His people from judgment. The very Hebrew word translated "pitch," in Genesis 6:14, is rendered "atonement," in Leviticus 17:11. It is the atonement that makes the believer safe in Christ as it was the pitch that made Noah and his family safe in the ark. By the use of symbolism it might also be assumed that Enoch is a type of the Church translated before judgment, while Noah is a type of Israel saved through judgment!

† Before us we have a book that presents the post-tribulation view. Its author states that the word translated "taken," in Matthew 24:40, 41, and in a parallel passage, Luke 17:34-36, the Greek verb *paralambanoo*, means *to take home, receive.* According to Liddell & Scott, in their *Greek-English Lexicon* (Oxford University Press) which this same commentator praises quite highly, *to take home* is not included among the definitions of *paralambanoo*. *To receive* is correct, but here are some other definitions of the same verb: *to take, to undertake, to associate with oneself, to seize, to take by force, to take prisoner.* Some of these definitions are far removed from *to take home.* The word is found at least twice in Matthew, other than the instance before us: (1) in 4:5: "Then the devil *taketh* Him up into the holy city"; and (2) in 27:27: "Then the soldiers of the governor *took* Jesus into the common hall." Assuredly in neither of these cases is the signification of the verb that of *taking home.*

who were left were left to live on earth. That is just the reverse order of how it will be at the translation of the Church, when those who are taken will be taken to be with Christ, while those who are left will be left on earth for judgment.

The allusion is most certainly to the time of the coming of the Son of man in power and glory. That coming is unquestionably after the Tribulation. The circumstances of the taking of the one from the field or from the grinding mill, and the leaving of the other, connected as they are with Noah's day, do not relate to the Rapture at all, unless we err grievously. It is quite true that, when the translation of the Church occurs, one will be taken while another will be left; but, as we have already observed, those taken then will be caught up into heaven, and those left then will be left on earth. This passage cannot be used as a proof text that the Church will pass through the Tribulation. It has to do with those who are on earth when Christ returns to the earth—those taken will be those who have rejected God and His Christ; those left will be tribulation-saints, Israel primarily, who will enter the earthly kingdom.

We see no reference to resurrection in the allusion to and comparison with Noah's days. But unless there is resurrection there is no rapture. Those who are left on earth, when this prophecy is fulfilled, will be that remnant of Israel which will turn to Messiah in that day. Jeremiah wrote concerning them: "And these are the words that the Lord spake concerning Israel . . . For thus saith the Lord; We have heard a voice of trembling, of fear, and not of peace. . . . Alas! for that day is great, so that none is like it: it is even the time of Jacob's trouble; but he shall be saved out of it. . . . Therefore fear thou not, O My servant Jacob, saith the Lord; neither be dismayed, O Israel: for, lo, I will save thee from afar, and thy seed from the land of their captivity; and Jacob shall return, and shall be in rest, and be quiet, and none shall make him afraid" (Jer. 30:4-10).

The final prophecy of the Olivet Discourse relates again to the coming of the Lord Jesus Christ after the Tribulation: "When the Son of man shall come in His glory, and all the holy angels with Him, then shall He sit upon the throne of His glory: and before Him shall be gathered all nations: and He shall separate them one from another, as a shepherd divideth his sheep from the goats: and He shall set the sheep on His right hand, but the goats on the left. Then shall the King say unto them on His right hand, Come, ye blessed of My Father, inherit the kingdom prepared for you from the foundation of the world. . . . Then shall He say also unto them on the left hand, Depart from Me, ye cursed, into everlasting fire, prepared for the devil and his angels. . . . And these shall go away into everlasting punishment; but the righteous into life eternal" (Matt. 25:31–46).

This whole scene is earthly. It is what is known as the judgment of the nations; the sheep are those who show mercy to them whom the Lord Jesus calls, "these My brethren" (vs. 40); and the goats are those who are deficient in exercising such mercy. The gracious reward given to the sheep is entrance into "the kingdom prepared for you from the foundation of the world" (vs. 34), and life eternal (vs. 46); the righteous judgment that falls on the goats is everlasting punishment (vs. 46). In no sense, when the nations are judged as to their treatment of Israel, are we to suppose that one whole nation will be numbered among either the sheep or the goats. The nations are the Gentiles, in contrast with the Jews. Some of the Gentiles from every nation, doubtless, will be numbered among the sheep, and some among the goats. The scene is not in the clouds or in heaven, but on earth.

In proposing that the parable of the sheep and the goats speaks of the Rapture, the post-tribulationists raise for themselves a question that they must find it difficult to answer, namely: Who will be left on earth to enter the Millennium if the parable of the sheep and the goats refers to the Rapture? For if the sheep represent the Church, all of the sheep must be translated at that time; and, in view of the fact that the goats are all to be consigned upon that occasion to "everlasting fire, prepared for the devil and his angels" (vs. 41), there will be no one left to partake of millennial blessedness on this earth.

The Church is not in this parable. The Church, a body of believers in Christ "chosen . . . in Him *before* the foundation of the world" (Eph. 1:4), is called to "an inheritance incorruptible, and undefiled, that fadeth not away, reserved *in heaven*" (I Pet. 1:4). The sheep of Matthew 25 are evidently called "to inherit the kingdom prepared . . . from the foundation of the world" (vs. 34), *an earthly kingdom,* the kingdom of David and David's greater Son. Furthermore, there is no resurrection here, and without the resurrection there is no rapture.

One other passage in the Gospels ought to be considered before we examine the teaching of the epistles. It is a portion of Scripture which, according to one of our post-tribulation brethren, "spells midnight" to the doctrine of the pre-tribulation rapture of the Church. What he alludes to is the parable of the wheat and the tares, found in Matthew 13:24–30, 36–43.

Briefly, the mystery parables of Matthew 13 have to do with Christendom during our Lord's absence from this earth. These parables do not refer to the Messianic kingdom that John the Baptist preached and our Lord presented in His early ministry on earth, for the parables are clearly said to pertain to things "kept secret from the foundation of the world" (vs. 35). The parables do not depict the Church as Christ's body in view of the fact that, within the orb of this kingdom of the heavens, are tares, children of Satan (vss. 38, 39). Christendom, then, the sphere of professing Christianity, is that which is designated in the parables of this chapter pertaining to the mysteries of the kingdom of the heavens.

In the parable of the wheat and the tares we see believers in Christ, known as children of the kingdom, represented by the wheat; and children of the wicked one, Satan, depicted by the tares (vs. 38). At the end of the age, the Lord Jesus said in explaining the parable to His disciples, "the Son of man shall send forth His angels, and they shall gather out of His kingdom [that is, Christendom] all things that offend, and them which do iniquity; and shall cast them into a furnace of fire. . . . Then shall the righteous shine forth as the sun in the kingdom of their Father" (vss. 41–43). The tares are not to be gathered up before the harvest, the end of the age, lest the wheat might be rooted up at the same time. Both are to grow together until the harvest (vss. 28–30).

The question is asked: "Since both the wheat and the tares are to grow together until the harvest, the end of the age, by what authority can anyone declare that the Rapture will take place seven years, or three and one-half years, or a period of any duration whatever, prior to the end of the age?" And it is further argued that the disposition of both the wheat and the tares must be concurrent. But do our post-tribulation friends, we ask in reply, act wholly in accord with what they demand of us? The parable tells us: "Gather ye together *first* the tares, and bind them in bundles to burn them: but gather the wheat into my barn" (vs. 30). It is the premise of most of those who believe that the Church will go through the Tribulation, that the rapture of the Church will take place as the Lord is returning to the earth, so that the Church will meet the Lord in the air on His way to earth and will come back with Him. But that would be the gathering of the wheat prior to the binding of the tares, the exact reverse of the order given in the parable.

It is important to note that it is the tares, rather than the wheat, that the servants are told not to gather before the harvest, lest, in so doing, some of the wheat might be rooted up also. Be that as it may, both grow together until the end of the age. No one supposes, however, that every stem or ear of wheat, that is, every believer in Christ, is to live on earth until the harvest, the end of the age; or that every blade of darnel, children of the wicked one, will live out the age. Some die every day. But corporately they will grow together till the end. When the harvest comes there will be both wheat and tares to be gathered.

We do not see the Rapture in this parable. There is no resurrection here and, as our post-tribulation friends remind us, where the Rapture is there must also be resurrection. Rather, we believe that this has to do with the very separation of the righteous and the unrighteous that is spoken of in the prophecy of the judgment of the sheep and the goats (Matt. 25:31–46). Even after the Church, the body of Christ, is gone, the apostate ecclesiastical organization will remain in Christendom, and this will comprise, for the most part, the children of the wicked one. Even after the Church, as a body, is gone, through the calling and sealing of the 144,000 and the great multitude of Revelation 7, there will be children of the kingdom on earth, and it is they who will be gathered to shine forth in the kingdom of their Father.

"But what did the listeners to the mystery parables of Matthew 13 know about Revelation 7?" someone will ask. They knew nothing about it, quite obviously. But they had no need of knowing; they knew nothing about the Rapture either, for it was not yet revealed. But the resurrection was a truth which all of them *had been taught;* and yet the resurrection is not spoken of here.

We should be dishonest if we did not admit that this parable, even after its interpretation by our Lord Himself, presents certain difficulties and that all do not agree as to some details of its fulfilment.* Yet one thing seems reasonably evident: the

---

* There is disagreement among the post-tribulationists no less than among the pre-tribulationists. For example, some suggest that the Lord

gathering of the wheat, *after* the tares are bound for burning, does not depict the Rapture which, whether before or after the Tribulation, *must precede* our Lord's destruction of His enemies, since, when He comes back to the earth, He will bring His saints with Him (Col. 3:4; I Thess. 3:13; Jude 14, 15; etc.).

---

will translate His saints on the way to the earth, as He returns to judge and reign; others submit that it will be after this, and that the saints whom He brings with Him, when He comes, are the Old Testament saints only. Or again, one writer declares that John 14:3 alludes to the translation of the Church; while another says that it does not but has to do with our Lord's receiving His own, one by one, as they die during this present age. It is not disagreements between brethren that we are seeking to point out in this series of articles, however; we are tracing what the Scriptures teach on the subject under consideration. Doubtless all of us will find, when we are with Christ, that we have erred in some measure!

CHAPTER VI

THE WRATH TO COME

The Thessalonian epistles are distinctly communications that pertain to the return of the Lord Jesus Christ. In both letters the second advent is mentioned in every chapter, in some instances in relation to Christ's coming for His Church, and in others, in respect to His return to the earth in power and glory. No examination of what the Scriptures teach as to the time of the translation of the Church in relation to the Tribulation, is complete, therefore, without an analysis of Paul's two letters to the saints at Thessalonica.

We shall discuss the First Epistle in this chapter.

Chapter 1 ends with the familiar commendation of the Thessalonian believers because they had "turned to God from idols to serve the living and true God; and to wait for His Son from heaven, whom He raised from the dead, even Jesus, who delivered us from the wrath to come" (vss. 9, 10). Ardent pre-tribulationists insist that "the wrath to come," here alluded to, is the wrath of the Lamb and of God, spoken of a number of times in The Revelation (see, e.g., **6**:16, 17; **15**:1; etc.), which is to fall upon mankind on this earth. Equally zealous post-tribulationists deny that "the wrath to come," here mentioned, has any reference to the wrath of God that is to assail this earth but propose, rather, that the expression, in I Thessalonians 1:10, alludes to "the wrath of God" that abides upon those who do not believe on the Son of God (John **3**:36), God's eternal wrath that will express itself in the eternal judgment of sinners who reject the Saviour. There is something to be said for both viewpoints.

The Greek verb *rhuomai,* translated "delivered" in the King

James Version, is actually in the present participle here: *ton rhuomenon*. Thus the clause would be better rendered: "who is delivering us from the wrath to come." We do not see any proof for either view. Consequently, so as to be wholly fair to our post-tribulation friends, we shall concede that they may be correct in this instance.

The Thessalonian believers were waiting for God's Son from heaven. Had He come in their day, they would have been caught up into His presence, to be sure. But insofar as we know, to this point in the epistle they were uninformed as to the Rapture. They were waiting for the Lord to come from heaven but they were not aware of what His coming involved.

Chapters 2:19 and 3:13 refer, as almost all will agree, to Christ's return to the earth to judge and to reign, when He will bring His blood-purchased saints with Him. These two passages, therefore, do not bear upon the theme of these studies.

Concerning chapter 4:13–18, there is general agreement among students of the Word, all concurring that the Rapture is here described.

It is this writer's opinion that verse 14 alludes to Christ's return *to the earth*. It states that God will bring with Him, when He comes again, those who now "sleep in Jesus." How can this be? How will God bring them back to the earth with the Lord Jesus, since their bodies are now in the grave? Verses 15–17 reveal this to us: "For this we say unto you by the Word of the Lord, that we which are alive and remain unto the coming of the Lord shall not precede them which are asleep. For the Lord Himself shall descend from heaven with a shout, with the voice of the archangel, and with the trump of God: and the dead in Christ shall rise first: then we which are alive and remain shall be caught up together with them in the clouds, to meet the Lord in the air: and so shall we ever be with the Lord." This is the translation of the Church, and here, with

the up-calling of living believers, we find the resurrection of
the righteous dead.

"Wherefore comfort one another with these words" (vs. 18).
Indeed, it is comfort; it is the blessed hope of the Church.

While this is the most detailed description of the saint's translation that is written in the Scripture, nothing is said here, as
all will agree, as to when this will happen in relation to the
Tribulation.

Chapter 5 opens with a long dissertation concerning the
coming of the Lord. "But of the times and seasons, brethren,
ye have no need that I write unto you. For yourselves know
perfectly that the day of the Lord so cometh as a thief in the
night. For when they shall say, Peace and safety; then sudden
destruction cometh upon them, as travail upon a woman with
child; and they shall not escape. But ye, brethren, are not in
darkness, that that day should overtake you as a thief. Ye are
all the children of light, and the children of the day; we are
not of the night, nor of darkness. Therefore, let us not sleep,
as do others; but let us watch and be sober. For they that sleep
sleep in the night; and they that be drunken are drunken in the
night. But let us, who are of the day, be sober, putting on the
breastplate of faith and love; and for an helmet, the hope of
salvation. For God hath not appointed us to wrath, but to obtain salvation by our Lord Jesus Christ, who died for us, that,
whether we wake or sleep, we should live together with Him.
Wherefore comfort yourselves together, and edify one another,
even as also ye do" (I Thess. 5:1–11).

Our brethren, who hold and teach that the Church will be
on the earth during all or a part of the Tribulation, make
much of this passage of Scripture. Their postulations may be
summarized briefly as follows: (1) there were no chapter divisions when this letter was written, and here, in chapter 5,
we have a clear indication of the time, in relation to the Tribulation, of the rapture of the Church of whose translation

chapter 4 tells us; (2) if the apostle had intended to indicate that the day of the Lord would not come upon the Church on earth, he would have left out, in verse 4, the words, "as a thief," and would simply have stated: "But ye, brethren, are not in darkness, that that day should overtake you"; and (3) the wrath, spoken of in verse 9, to which believers are said not to have been appointed, is the same wrath as spoken of in chapter 1:10 and is, therefore, the wrath of John 3:36, eternal wrath in judgment upon those who die in unbelief. Suppose we examine these propositions.

(1) Quite obviously, chapter divisions were not in the original manuscripts. This fact does not, however, prove that the events spoken of in chapter 5 apply directly to that which is recorded at the end of chapter 4. There may be direct relationship between the two but there need not be. On the other hand, the expression, "the day of the Lord" (vs. 2), identifies the description that follows with God's dealings with men on earth. The term is used throughout the Old Testament to signify a time when the Lord, Messiah, will come to judge and reign. It is predicted as falling upon the proud and lofty, those lifted high in their own conceits, the disobedient and ungodly, etc. (see, e.g., Isa. 2:10-22; Amos 5:18-20; Zeph. 1:14-18).* It is not said to be a time of resurrection; yet where the Rapture is, there is resurrection.

(2) It is true that the apostle, in speaking of the coming day of the Lord, declares: "But ye, brethren, are not in darkness, that that day should overtake you *as a thief*" (vs. 4). The last three words can hardly be a proof-text, surely, that the day of the Lord will overtake the Church. The Lord will come to this earth in judgment "as a thief," that is, unexpectedly. He will

---

* It is of interest to observe, also, that the expression, "the times and the seasons" (vs. 1), is used elsewhere in Scripture to denote events that relate to earth and the establishment of kingdoms (Dan. 2:21, Acts 1:7).

not come upon His own as a thief, or unexpectedly; rather, He
will come as a bridegroom for his bride who will indeed be
expecting Him, yes, awaiting Him. Others, who do not know
the Lord, sleep, and are given over to debauchery; but *we,* the
Church of God, children of the light, children of the day, do
not sleep but are awake, watching in soberness for Him to
come and to take us to Himself.

(3) "For God hath not appointed us to wrath, but to obtain
salvation by our Lord Jesus Christ" (vs. 9). We cannot agree
that the wrath of verse 9 is descriptive particularly of that
which is spoken of in John 3:36, although that wrath is surely
included in what is alluded to here. For this is a divine principle: God has not appointed His own to wrath at any time—on
earth or in eternity—but to obtain salvation by our blessed
Lord.

Some will argue that the saints of all centuries have had
tribulation and that they have suffered wrath also. They will
point to the martyrs of Nero's day and other times, even of
today, and declare that God has never promised to protect His
people from trial.

That Christians must endure tribulation and persecution is
too well known to require proof. Yet, in order that our memories may be refreshed, let us recall several Scriptures as con-
firmation. Our Lord, while He was here on this earth in person, told His followers: "In the world ye shall have tribulation:
but be of good cheer; I have overcome the world" (John
16:33). The Apostle Paul warned us: "Yea, and all that will
live godly in Christ Jesus shall suffer persecution" (II Tim.
3:12). And in the very epistle under consideration, I Thessalonians, it is stated "that no man should be moved by these
afflictions: for yourselves know that we are appointed there-
unto" (3:3).

Tribulation, persecution, and affliction are the lot of those
who love and serve the Lord whom the world crucified. It

hated Him and it hates His people. But there is a vast difference between tribulation, or persecution, or affliction, and the wrath of God. Tribulation comes to us in this world, and is allowed of God; it may even come from Him as chastisement of us, so that we may grow thereby. "And not only so, but we glory in tribulations also: knowing that tribulation worketh patience; and patience, experience; and experience, hope: and hope maketh not ashamed" (Rom. 5:3, 4). Persecution, on the other hand, comes from the enemies of Christ and His cross; and our all-wise God permits us to bear it for His own glory. He will not suffer us to be tried above that which we are able to bear. He bestows grace in the time of need. He allows us, by the persecution that we undergo, to know something of the fellowship of Christ's sufferings (Phil. 3:10), and to "fill up that which is behind of the afflictions of Christ . . . for His body's sake, which is the Church" (Col. 1:24). And affliction, like the rain, falls upon the just and unjust alike. Yet naught can touch the child of God apart from His permissive will.

A beloved brother and very dear friend, writing from the post-tribulation position, states: "When we have on occasion warned that God's people must be prepared to suffer tribulation in the age-end since that is consistently declared to be the believer's portion, we have been flippantly answered by some devotee of the theory of pre-tribulation rapture, with the quotation: 'God hath not appointed us to wrath' (I Thess. 5:9). Indeed, beloved, He has not appointed us to wrath, but wrath is not tribulation and cannot be confused with tribulation without serious consequences." Not in any spirit of flippancy but with all earnestness and seriousness, we reply to our brother: Tribulation is not of necessity wrath, but the period known as "the Tribulation" is indeed the manifestation of the wrath of God. God's people will surely suffer tribulation during this age but the Church will not be obliged to endure *the* Tribulation, the time of the outpouring of God's wrath.

Never does the wrath of God come upon His own. "There is therefore now no condemnation to them which are in Christ Jesus" (Rom. 8:1). This is divine principle, as we have already stated. "For God hath not appointed us to wrath, but to obtain salvation by our Lord Jesus Christ." That the period of tribulation that is to come upon this world is as a result of the wrath of the Lamb and of God is asserted too frequently, in the book that deals in great part with the Tribulation, that is, The Revelation, to allow any doubt that this tribulation is not the kind alluded to in such passages as John 16:33 but a specific period when God's wrath will be poured out upon the world. He has not appointed His own to His wrath in any form.

"For God hath not appointed us to wrath, but to obtain salvation by our Lord Jesus Christ, who died for us, that, whether we wake or sleep, we should live together with Him." "Wherefore comfort yourselves together, and edify one another, even as also ye do."

CHAPTER VII

THAT DAY SHALL NOT COME EXCEPT—

In the quest for what the Scriptures reveal regarding the Church's translation in relation, in time, to the Tribulation, there are two passages in Second Thessalonians that require special attention. It may be necessary to become rather technical in our examination of these portions but the end, to seek to know the truth, assuredly justifies serious concentration.

Our post-tribulation brethren are quite strong in submitting that II Thessalonians 1:3–10, if carefully studied, "will dispel . . . from the minds of any who hold the Scripture as final authority, and not the cunningly devised fables of men," the idea that the Church will not go through the Tribulation. But is this so?

It is a well known fact that the second letter to the Thessalonians was written to these believers in Christ in order to correct certain confusion in their minds concerning the coming of the Lord in its relationship to themselves (2:2). After the apostolic greeting in chapter 1, the apostle expresses his thanks to God because of the growing faith and abounding love of these young Christians, and for their patience and faith in all their persecutions and tribulations (vss. 3, 4). He declares that this kind of endurance of such trials is the evident token of the righteous judgment of God, and that it is all connected with future blessedness in the kingdom of God (vs. 5). Then he adds: "Seeing it is a righteous thing with God to recompense tribulation to them that trouble you; and to you who are troubled rest with us, when the Lord Jesus shall be revealed from heaven with His mighty angels, in flaming fire taking vengeance on them that know not God, and that obey not the

Gospel of our Lord Jesus Christ: who shall be punished with everlasting destruction from the presence of the Lord, etc." (vss. 6–10).

Before we proceed further, it may be well to clarify an expression that is not wholly transparent in our English translations. The word rendered "rest" (Gr., *anesin*), in verse 7, is not a verb but a noun meaning *ease, relief,* and *relaxation,* as well as *rest.* If we rearrange slightly the construction of the sentence, the sense of the passage may be clearer: "Seeing it is a righteous thing with God to recompense tribulation to them that trouble you, and rest with us to you who are troubled."

"You are being persecuted and tried," says the apostle, "and your patience and faith throughout these tribulations are a manifest token of God's righteous judgment, so that you may be counted worthy of the kingdom of God; for it is for Him that you suffer. Never mind the present suffering! God's judgment is righteous. And it will be seen that it is a righteous thing with Him to repay—tribulation to them that trouble you, and rest with all His people to you who are troubled, in the revelation of Jesus Christ from heaven, when He shall take vengeance on them that know not God and His Christ, punishing them with everlasting destruction and separation from His presence, and when He shall be glorified in all His saints, and admired, wondered at, in all them that believe. Today you suffer, and those who trouble you are at ease. A day is coming when *they* will suffer eternal punishment, and *you,* who now suffer, will be released and glorified."

It would be decidedly unfair did we not acknowledge that our post-tribulationist friends have a strong point here, especially if the rendition of the Authorized Version is adhered to— that those troubling God's people will suffer tribulation, and those who are troubled will enjoy rest, *"when* the Lord Jesus shall be revealed from heaven with His mighty angels, taking vengeance on them that know not God. . . ." Were this the only Scripture on the subject of the relation, in time, of judgment upon wicked men on earth to blessing upon men of faith, we might readily conclude that the two divine acts of recompense will take place at one moment, in one hour, as it were. Actually, however, the Greek of verse 7 does not state, *"when the Lord Jesus shall be revealed, etc.,"* but "in the revelation of the Lord Jesus" (*en tee apokalupsei*), an expression that deignates more than the actual descent from heaven of our Lord Jesus Christ in power and great glory (see, i.e., Rev. 1:1). If we mistake not, it is not so much the moment that these things will occur that is the issue here but, rather, that at such a time as those who are now persecuting the Church are themselves recompensed with tribulation from God, those who are now troubled will be enjoying rest from sufferings.

Some have been confused by the use of the words, "tribulations" and "tribulation," in verses 4 and 6 respectively. This is not *the* Tribulation but simply affliction. The context makes this quite clear. It was specifically to repudiate such confusion in the minds of the Thessalonian Christians that this letter was written. They supposed that, because of the tribulation that they were experiencing, the day of the Lord had already come and that they were enduring the tribulation *of that day*. But no, the apostle assures them, this is not so. When the ungodly are suffering under the righteous judgment of God, His own people will be enjoying eternal rest.

The proposition is developed in chapter 2. "Now we beseech you, brethren," the apostle continues, "by the coming of our Lord Jesus Christ, and by our gathering together unto Him, that ye be not soon shaken in mind, or be troubled, neither by spirit, nor by word, nor by letter as from us, as that the day of the Lord is at hand" (vss. 1, 2).

It will be observed that we have changed the expression, "the day of Christ," of the Authorized Version, to "the day of the Lord," as in the Revised Version. Freely acknowledging that at least one of the ancient MSS gives authority for the translation, "the day of Christ," we affirm that "the day of the Lord" is correct.* And we cannot agree, as one of our post-tribulationist brethren states it, that "the expressions 'day of Christ' and 'day of the Lord' were interchangeable," and, that to teach that there is a difference is "misleading and false. . . . It is another one of the many meaningless and confusing hair-splittings which characterize the dispensational school." We are convinced that it makes a great deal of difference and that the expressions refer to two different events and are no more interchangeable than are the terms, "day of redemption" and "day of wrath."

The day of the Lord refers to the same time as the day of Jehovah in the Old Testament. It is a day of judgment, of destruction, of disaster, and of cataclysmic upheavals in the heavens (Isa. 13:9-11; Acts 2:20; I Thess. 5:2; II Pet. 3:10), which will issue in the righteous reign of Christ over this earth (Zech. 14). Wherever the expression is found in the New Testament, it is in connection with judgment. It seems to include the full tribulation period and not simply the occasion of our Lord's visible return in power.

On the other hand, that which we speak of as the day of Christ (and this includes every term wherein the names that the Son of God bore on earth, that is "Jesus," or "Christ," are employed; namely: the day of Christ, the day of Jesus Christ, the day of the Lord Jesus, and the day of the Lord Jesus Christ) invariably has reference to an occasion of salvation, rejoicing, or blessing (I Cor. 1:8; 5:5; II Cor. 1:14; Phil. 1:6, 10; 2:16). The expressions, "the day of the Lord" and "the day of Christ" are not synonymous at all.

---

* Even so ardent an anti-dispensationalist as the esteemed Dr. Oswald T. Allis says, in *Prophecy and the Church* (The Presbyterian and Reformed Publishing Company, Philadelphia), that the proper rendering is "the 'day of the Lord,' (not, 'day of Christ,' as in AV)."

By the very facts made known in the first epistle concerning the coming of our Lord Jesus Christ and our gathering together unto Him, that is, the Rapture as revealed in chapter 4, the Thessalonian Christians are told not to be shaken in mind, or troubled. Evidently a spurious message had come to them, purportedly from Paul, suggesting that the day of the Lord was "already present" (a better rendition than "at hand"). But the tribulation that they were enduring was not a part of God's wrath poured out upon the world. It was persecution from man. God would recompense the offenders with judgment, and those who were being troubled, with rest. Therefore, by the very hope of Christ's coming and the gathering together of the saints unto Him, they could be sure that the day of the Lord was not yet present. Certain things must take place before that day would come, circumstances that had not yet occurred. The nature of these things is revealed in the verses that follow.

"Let no man deceive you by any means," says Paul, "for that day shall not come, except there come a falling away first, and that man of sin be revealed, the son of perdition . . . Remember ye not, that, when I was yet with you, I told you these things?" (vss. 3–5).

Two events must occur, and in a specific order, before the day of the Lord: (1) the (the definite article, *hee,* is in the Greek) falling away; and (2) the revelation of the man of sin. It is the former of these two phenomena that we would discuss as pertaining to the subject of this treatise.

We suggest, for prayerful deliberation, a deviation from the accepted translation and interpretation of this passage. It is never the part of wisdom, we believe, to discard traditional renditions of the ancient MSS unless we have reasonable proof to support our views. We shall, therefore, present, for consideration, such evidence as we are able to produce.

The Greek words, translated "a falling away," are *hee*

apostasia. It is directly from the noun that we obtain our English word *"apostasy."* *Apostasia* generally carries the meaning of *defection, revolt,* or *rebellion against God.* These are the primary meanings of the word, as found in most lexicons. There is a secondary connotation in Liddell & Scott's *Greek-English Lexicon,** namely: *disappearance,* or *departure.*

In determining the true meaning of a word in the Bible, we must discover its customary usage in the Scriptures. The noun, *apostasia,* occurs in only one other instance in the New Testament, that is, in Acts 21:21, where Paul is accused of teaching the Jews to "forsake Moses," and this assuredly is related to rebellion against God.

Apostasia, or an older form of the noun, *apostasis,* is found frequently in the *Septuagint* (the Greek translation of the Old Testament): Josh. 22:22; I Kings 21:13; II Chron. 29:19; 33:19; Isa. 30:1; and Jer. 2:19. Its usage in these passages has to do with departure from God. It is well to bear in mind, however, that in every instance either a descriptive phrase so signifying, or the context in which the word is employed, particularizes its meaning. Having said these things in favor of the traditional translation of *apostasia,* let us look further.

It is from the verb that we obtain the root meaning of a noun. *Apostasia,* the noun, comes from the verb *aphisteemi,* which means *to remove,* or, in the causal sense, *to put away,* or *to cause to be removed.* This root verb, *aphisteemi,* is used fifteen times in the New Testament: Luke 2:27; 4:13; 8:13; 22:29; Acts 5:37, 38; 12:10; 15:38; 19:9; 22:29; II Cor. 12:8; I Tim. 4:1; 6:5; II Tim. 2:19; and Heb. 3:12. Of these fifteen occurrences of the verb, only three have any reference to religious departure. In all three of these cases, by context (Luke 8:13), and by the descriptive phrases, "from the faith" and

---

* New Edition, Jones & McKenzie (Oxford University Press, New York). While this lexicon pertains to Classic Greek rather than to New Testament Greek, this fact in no way detracts from its authority in respect to the root meaning of words.

"from the living God" respectively (I Tim. 4:1; Heb. 3:12), religious defection is designated. In eleven of the fifteen N. T. occurrences, the actual word "depart" is used in translating *aphisteemi*, in relation to such modes of departure as that of the angel who, having delivered Peter from prison, *"departed from him"* (Acts 12:10), and of Paul's prayer that his thorn in the flesh "might *depart"* from him (II Cor. 12:8).

It is evident, then, that the verb *aphisteemi* does have the meaning of *to depart* in the New Testament, in a very general sense which is not specialized as being related to rebellion against God or forsaking the faith. And, since a noun takes its meaning from the verb, the noun, too, may have such a broad connotation. "The departure" is assuredly an acceptable translation of *hee apostasia** and is, in our opinion, the proper one.

The day of the Lord will not come, then, until the man of sin be revealed. And before he is revealed, there must be "the departure." Departure from what or to what? It must have been something concerning which the Thessalonian believers were informed, else the definite article would hardly have been employed, and without any qualifying description with the noun.† *Why do we assume that this departure must be from the faith?* It has been shown that, in its verb form, the word frequently signifies separation other than religious revolt. Have we not based our interpretation upon what may quite possibly be an inappropriate rendition of the Greek noun? And since the definite article suggests strongly that the departure was something with which the Thessalonians were familiar, why do we think of the departure as apostasy? There is nothing in

---

* William Tyndale's version of the N. T., translated and published at Worms, c. 1526, renders *hee apostasia,* "a departynge." Coverdale (A.D. 1535), Cranmer (1539), and the Geneva Bible (1557) render it the same way. Beza (1565) translates *apostasia* "departing."

† Such a noted scholar as Dr. George Milligan, in his commentary on the Greek text (Macmillan, New York), although holding to the traditional translation of *apostasia*, states that "the use of the definite article proves [that the *apostasia* referred to is one] regarding which the apostle's readers were already fully informed."

either of the Thessalonian espistles, to this point, about the great apostasy. To submit that, while the apostle did not write to this church about the apostasy he must have talked to them about it, is pure conjecture.

Again, how would the Thessalonians, or Christians in any century since, be qualified to recognize the apostasy when it should come, assuming, simply for the sake of this inquiry, that the Church might be on earth when it does come? There has been apostasy from God, rebellion against Him, since time began. And if it be proposed that the man of sin, sitting in the temple of God and showing Himself to be God, is *the* apostasy, we must ask ourselves a question: Is this act, on the part of the man of sin, apostasy, a falling away, or is it blasphemous denial by one who never at any time acknowledged God?

There is a departure concerning which the Thessalonians had been instructed by letter. This is not conjecture but fact: it is the rapture of the Church, described in I Thessalonians 4:13–17. It was on account of the confusion in the minds of these young Christians, in the matter of events associated with the coming of the Lord, that this epistle was written—for some had sought to deceive them, as by spirit (claiming, perhaps, some new revelation from God), or by word (possibly a misinterpretation of something Paul said), or by letter as from Paul, telling the Thessalonians that the day of the Lord was already present. And how could the apostle set their minds at rest? He could assure them, "by the coming of our Lord Jesus Christ, and by our gathering together unto Him," that the day of the Lord will not come "except there come the departure, the Rapture, first, and that man of sin be revealed, the son of perdition." The day of the Lord was not present; for they themselves, members of Christ's mystical body, were still on earth. The Rapture had not already taken place, they being left behind; for the man of sin was not revealed.

This interpretation corresponds perfectly, in sequence, with

that in verses 7 and 8, if the restraining power is, as we believe
to be the case, the Holy Spirit. The Church departs, and the
man of sin is revealed (vs. 3); the Holy Spirit, the restrainer, is
taken out of the way, "and then shall that wicked one be revealed" (vss. 7, 8).

It would be entirely inappropriate for us to be dogmatic in a
matter so involved and still open to question as that which we
have been discussing. We have expressed our understanding of
the passage as fully as we are able. We are persuaded, in our
own mind, that this is the correct view of this passage. If we
are not mistaken, we have here a final answer to the time of
the translation of the Church in relation to the Tribulation.
However, if we do err, it does not alter the other truths that
we have sought to bring out to this point, and still others
which we shall seek to point out in the chapters that follow.*

---

* After this study of the early verses of II Thessalonians 2 appeared
in *Our Hope,* one of our post-tribulation brethren in England published a criticism of it, in which he stated that (1) the "novel idea"
of rendering *hee apostasia* as "the departure" reverses the meaning
of the inspired Word and is very much like "wresting the Scripture";
and (2) that "any moment rapture teaching must be in a sorry case
for support, if it turns to such twisting of terms."
But our British friend misses the point.
(1) To translate *hee apostasia* as "the departure" is not a "novel
idea" at all, since it dates back to the 16th Century, as has been
shown. There is absolutely no doubt that *hee apostasia* can properly
be rendered "the departure." That about which there is a reasonable
question is whether "the departure" may properly be interpreted
to refer to the rapture of the church, or whether it must allude to the
apostasy, which is the generally accepted interpretation.
(2) The author did not twist the meaning of the Scripture so
that he might arrive at a conclusion favorable to the pre-tribulation
position. Some question had arisen in his own mind as to whether
the Church would or would not pass through the Tribulation, and
II Thessalonians 2 was the first Scripture portion that he examined
to discover for himself what the Bible teaches on this whole subject.
In the study of this passage he reached the conclusion that has
been presented in this chapter. He has been careful to state (a) that
he considers it inappropriate to be dogmatic about an interpretation
that is still open to question; and (b) that the pre-tribulation interpretation does not rest, in his opinion, upon any one passage of the
Bible but upon a number of Scriptures which are discussed in this
volume.

CHAPTER VIII

THE RESTRAINER

We come now to that extremely puzzling passage of Scripture that has been a thorn in the flesh of many an expositor, namely, II Thessalonians 2:6–8. In the Authorized Version it is rendered: "And now ye know what withholdeth that he [the man of sin, vss. 3, 4] might be revealed in his time. For the mystery of iniquity doth already work: only he who now letteth will let, until he be taken out of the way. And then shall that Wicked be revealed, whom the Lord shall consume with the spirit of His mouth, and shall destroy with the brightness of His coming." It is verses 6 and 7 that pose the problem, and their interpretations have been legion. Who is the one who lets, that is, who hinders? Is the restrainer a person or an influence? Is that which withholds supernatural or natural?

One of our post-tribulationist brethren, writing about this Scripture, speaks of verse 7 as "the Golden Text of the advocates of the pre-tribulation rapture." This is because of the fact that most of those who believe that the Church will be translated before the Tribulation understand the restrainer, here spoken of, to be the Holy Spirit. It is stated that the restrainer is to "be taken out of the way." In view of the fact that the Spirit resides within the believer in Christ as a seal "unto the day of redemption" who will continue His work in the Christian "until the day of Jesus Christ" (Eph. 4:30; Phil. 1:6), it seems quite obvious that it is the Holy Spirit who restrains lawlessness through Christians who are the light of the world (Phil. 2:15; cf. Matt. 5:14). The restrainer will be "taken out of the way" in the day of Jesus Christ, the day when the Church is raptured. This is good logic *provided* it is established that the withholder, or hinderer, is the Holy Spirit.

It is not entirely accurate, in our opinion, to speak of this passage of Scripture as "the Golden Text of the advocates of the pre-tribulation rapture." There are not a few who hold that the Church will not pass through the Tribulation who do not teach that the restrainer is the Holy Spirit. For example, C. F. Hogg and W. E. Vine state, in their volume, *The Epistles of Paul the Apostle to the Thessalonians,* that the restrainer of this passage is Gentile dominion during the times of the Gentiles, as the constituted government ordained by God. And there are others of the same school who suggest variations of this interpretation, or that the restrainer is Satan. On the other hand, if II Thessalonians 2:6–8 is to be termed "the Golden text" of the advocates of any system of interpretation, we should suppose that it belongs to those who hold the post-tribulation view. At least, insofar as we are concerned, we do not recall having read the writings of a single post-tribulationist who does not insist very definitely that the restrainer is *not* the Holy Spirit.

The exegesis of these verses is admittedly one of the most difficult in all the Bible. Suppose we examine the text and the various interpretations of it, to learn what we can about it.

The apostle has been speaking, in verses 3 (last clause) and 4, of the revelation of the man of sin and what his activities will be. Paul reminds his readers that, when he was yet with them, he told them these things (vs. 5). And now he discloses why it is that the man of sin has, up to this time, been kept back: "And now ye know what withholdeth that he might be revealed in his time. For the mystery of lawlessness doth already work: only he who now hindereth will continue to hinder, until he be taken out of the way" (vs. 6, 7). We have made two changes in the text as it is rendered in the Authorized Version. "Lawlessness" is a better translation of the Greek, *tees anomias,* than "iniquity," and expresses the exact antithesis to the principle of order and righteousness. As to the substitution of "hindereth" for "letteth," it is due to the fact that the English word, "let," has undergone a change in meaning since 1611, when the King James translation was issued. The Greek verb, *katechoo,* means *to hinder, to restrain.*

It seems quite evident also that there is a supernatural element in this lawlessness and its restraint at the present time on account of the appearance of the word "mystery," which is employed in the New Testament in relation to truths that were previously hidden but now, in connection with the use of the word, are divinely revealed (cf. Matt. 13:11; Rom. 16:25, 26; I Cor. 15:51; Eph. 3:3–5; etc.). So far what we have said is generally agreed upon, but this is not so in the case of that which follows.

The two problems that linguists and exegetes have puzzled over, and concerning which there have always been divergent views, are (1) the identity of the hinderer, or restrainer; and (2) the lot or destiny of the restrainer. The majority of the pre-tribulationists believes that the restrainer is the Holy Spirit, and that He will be taken out of the way when the Church is raptured. With this we agree. However, it is essential for us to do more than make an arbitrary assertion to that effect; we must be ready to give a reason for the hope that is in us.

In an effort to try to discover the true meaning of this passage, then, it will be expedient for us to delineate the most prominent viewpoints concerning it, to examine the possible translations of the text, and then to select the interpretation that offers the fewest difficulties. Once again it will be necessary for us to be somewhat technical in pursuing our investigation, but serious thought will not be harmful to any one of us. The study should be profitable.

There are four major viewpoints as to the identity of the restrainer: (1) it is the Roman Empire, or some modification of that empire, known as human government; (2) it is Gentile world-dominion; (3) it is Satan; and (4) it is the Holy Spirit. Lexically, any one of the four interpretations may obtain. In verse 6, the restrainer, "what withholdeth," is translated from the noun *to katechon* (neuter), and in verse 7 the restrainer, "he who hindereth," comes over from the noun *ho katechoon* (masculine). The different genders appear to signify an influence (in the neuter) and a personality (in the masculine). Such usage might apply to any of those generally identified as the restrainer: it may apply to a government, in verse 6, and to the head of that government, in verse 7; it may indicate satanic influence, in verse 6, and Satan himself, in verse 7; and it may apply to the divine influence of the Spirit in verse 6, and to the Holy Spirit Himself, in verse 7.

One expositor, an ardent post-tribulationist, who teaches that Satan is the restrainer, makes much of the fact that the intensive pronoun, *auton,* in verse 6, is in the masculine gender. He suggests that the usage of a masculine pronoun with a neuter antecedent, *to katechon,* makes it plain "that the Personality who is now withholding himself, is exactly the same power and personality who will reveal himself *'in his own season.'* He is not restraining the course of evil in this world," says this writer, "he is simply withholding himself from his personal manifestation until the psychological moment when lawlessness is ripe and 'transgressors are come to the full'." But does the masculine pronoun, *auton,* have a neuter antecedent? Why not a masculine antecedent, namely, "the man of sin . . . the son of perdition," of verse 3?

While it is true that, linguistically, any of the four proposed interpretations may be correct, this does not settle the matter. *Three of the interpretations must be erroneous since there can only be one true interpretation of any Scripture.* We must investigate further.

The final clause of verse 7 requires our attention. It is rendered "until he be taken out of the way," in the Authorized,

Revised, American Standard, and Douay Versions, etc., and
"until he is out of the way," in the Revised Standard Version.
This translation lends itself freely to our pre-tribulation interpretation that the restrainer is the Holy Spirit.

The same post-tribulationist brother whom we cited above,
in his sincere prosecution of positively identifying the restrainer
as Satan, maintains that " 'until he be taken out of the way'
. . . is the *exact opposite* of the true meaning" of the last clause
of verse 7.

The Greek is *heoos ek mesou geneetai. Heoos* means *until,*
and *ek mesou, out of the midst,* or *out of the way,* as any
Greek-English lexicon will show. It is the verb, *geneetai,* which
is the third personal, singular, second aorist, subjunctive of the
verb, *ginomai,* that presents the problem. Says our friend concerning this verb: "The word here translated 'taken' is the
Greek *ginomai,* meaning 'to become,' i.e., 'to come into existence, begin to be, receive being,' (Thayer's *first* definition),
otherwise 'to be appointed, constituted, established.' *There is
no* suggestion of a *removal,* but a *coming into* being. It is *the
same word used in connection with the incarnation of Christ,*
'The Word BECAME flesh,' etc. (John 1:14). Beloved saints
of God," this writer continues, "it is *not* the Holy Spirit in the
church being *removed* from the earth, it is the *coming into
being* from the midst of the earth, of Anti-christ, the *alter ego*
of Satan, who has been *withholding* himself until lawlessness,
man-glorification and wickedness are so rife and rampant that
they will 'wonder after' and 'worship' the Beast, whom he
brings up from the abyss in the midst of the earth (Rev.
17:8)."

It is quite true that Thayer's first definition of *ginomai* is
*to become, to come into existence, to begin to be, to receive
being.* It is also factual that this very verb is used in connection
with the Word becoming flesh, in John 1:14. The eternal Son,
the Word of God, did not come into existence, or begin to be,

or receive being, but he did *become* flesh. But why does this writer not tell us, since he uses Thayer as source material to discover the meaning of *ginomai,* that this same lexicographer, under the same word, *ginomai,* gives, for the idiomatic meaning of the verb with *ek mesou,* as the II Thessalonians 2:7: *to be taken out of the way?* And why does he fail to inform us that this same lexicographer, Thayer, under his definition of *mesos,* says: *"ginomai ek mesou,* to be taken out of the way, to disappear (II Thess. 2:7)"?

Ginomai alone has many meanings. We have traced through the New Testament to find that the word is used in various forms 621 times, and is translated in 49 different ways. It is rendered *to be, to be made, to come, to come to pass, to arise, to be assembled, to be brought, to be divided, to be finished, to be fulfilled, to be kept, to be ordained to be, to be married, to be performed, to be preferred, to be taken,* etc. It is rather difficult, therefore, to determine with finality its exact meaning. Yet practically every translator of the New Testament gives it the connotation, with *ek mesou,* of *to be taken out of the way,* or *to be removed.**

Tracing its use carefully, it is evident that *ginomai,* though exceedingly flexible, frequently suggests a change of something from one state to another: "the Word *became* flesh" (John 1:14); "stones *be made* bread" (Matt. 4:3); "the stone which the builders rejected, the same *is become* the head of the corner" (Matt. 21:42); etc.; or something that is completed: "the works *were finished* from the foundation of the world" (Heb. 4:3).

If we render *ek mesou geneetai,* quite literally, "out of the midst he become to be," it does not make much sense. But if

---

* Thus the phrase, *ek mesou gignesthai* is illustrated by Wetstein and Kypke (*Obs.,* Vol. II, page 343) as indicating "the removal of any obstacle, of anything . . . leaving the manner of removal wholly undefined; comp. *arthee ek mesou humoon,* I Cor. 5:2."

we remember the idiomatic use of the verb with *ek mesou,* and if we bear in mind also its suggestion of a change from one state to another, we may, with fair reasonableness, translate the clause, *heoos ek mesou geneetai:* "until he become from the midst," or "until he be taken out of the way."

Lexically, then, (a) in respect to the identity of the restrainer of verses 6 and 7, any one of the four postulations may obtain, that (1) the restrainer is the Roman Empire or some modified form of human government; (2) the restrainer is Gentile world-dominion; (3) the restrainer is Satan; and (4) the restrainer is the Holy Spirit; and (b) in respect to the proper rendition of the last clause of verse 7, while he who proposes that the verb *ginomai* must carry the meaning here of *coming into being* argues well, there is insufficient evidence to cause us to discard the accepted translation, "until he be taken out of the way."

Exegetically, we must dismiss immediately the proposition that the restrainer is the Roman Empire. This empire has long since ceased to exist and, although it is to be restored, assuredly it has not restrained evil for the past thousand and more years, nor is it a restrainer now. Neither can it be demonstrated that the restrainer is human government. While it is true that "the powers that be are ordained of God" (Rom. 13:1), the use of the word, "mystery," in view of its usual association with supernatural revelation or activity, appears to eliminate the rule of man as the restraining influence. Again, history discloses that human government, far from being a constant restraint against lawlessness, has itself been, upon occasion, lawless in relation to both God and society. And, furthermore, human government will not be removed when the man of sin is revealed, for he himself will be the most powerful dictator the world has ever known, under whose dominion no man will be able either to buy or to sell unless he has his mark upon him (Rev. 13:15–17).

Gentile world-dominion does not, in our opinion, fit the case any better than human government does, and for the same reasons generally.

As for Satan being the restrainer, when has he ever been a deterrence to evil? A house divided against itself cannot stand (Mark 3:25; cf. Luke 11:18). It is quite true that, in verse 6 of our passage, it is the man of sin whose revelation is restrained; however, in verse 7, it is lawlessness that is curbed, and Satan has never, insofar as we are aware, checked iniquity.

What of the Holy Spirit? Has He not, throughout this present age, been a restraining influence through the Church? We must not forget that our Lord said of His own: "Ye are the salt of the earth . . . Ye are the light of the world" (Matt. 5:13, 14). Salt prevents decay; light shines in the darkness and purifies. It has been the presence of God's people, indwelt by the Holy Spirit, that has been the restraining influence (*to katechon*, neuter). But when the Church is taken, the Holy Spirit (*ho katechoon*, masculine), will be removed as the restrainer. When He is thus taken out of the way, when the Church is gone, "then shall that Wicked be revealed, whom the Lord shall consume with the spirit of His mouth, and shall destroy with the brightness of His coming."

We are aware that the Spirit must work upon men during the Tribulation if any are to be saved then. But the fact that He is taken out of the way, as the indweller of believers in Christ, does not mean that He will not convict the world of sin, and of righteousness, and of judgment. The Holy Spirit has all the attributes of God; He is, therefore, omnipresent. It is only that phase of His ministry, as the abiding presence of Christ in the hearts of believers, that will cease when the Church is taken. As such, He now restrains lawlessness: "He who now restraineth will continue to restrain, until He be taken out of the way."

Admitting that the passage as a whole presents many diffi-

culties, it is our judgment that the interpretation that the restrainer is the Holy Spirit, who will "be taken out of the way"
when the Church is translated, not only offers fewer problems
than any other interpretation but is scriptural throughout,
logical, and reasonable. Moreover, the sequence presented in
verses 7 and 8 falls properly in line with that in verse 3. The
day of the Lord will not come, "except there come the departure [the Rapture] first, and that man of sin be revealed,
the son of perdition" (vs. 3); the mystery of lawlessness is
already working, "only He who now hinders will continue to
restrain, until He be taken out of the way. And then shall that
wicked one be revealed . . ." (vss. 7, 8).

The second chapter of II Thessalonians cannot be used as a
demonstration that the Church will pass through the Tribulation, even if some of our conclusions be erroneous. If we be
correct, however, the chapter offers unanswerable evidence
that, *before* the Tribulation can come, the Church *must* be
caught up to be with Christ.

CHAPTER IX

A JUDGE'S STAND AND A MARRIAGE SUPPER

There is general agreement between post-tribulationists and pre-tribulationists as to the fact that, when our Lord comes to the earth in power and great glory at the conclusion of the Tribulation, He will bring His raptured saints with Him. The Scriptures are quite explicit about this. Enoch, the seventh from Adam, predicted: "Behold, the Lord cometh with ten thousands of His saints" (Jude 14); and that the Church is included in this band is evident from Paul's declaration: "When Christ, who is our life, shall appear, then shall ye also appear with Him in glory" (Col. 3:4). Allusion is again made to this fact, if we mistake not, in I Thessalonians 4:14, where it is told that those who "sleep in Jesus will God bring *with* Him," that is, when He comes in glory; and verses 15–17 describe how this can come to pass. We have no doubt that the armies of Revelation 19:14, which are to accompany the returning King of kings and Lord of lords, include the saints, in view of the apparel designated.

Where the post-tribulationists and pre-tribulationists differ is in respect to the translation of the Church—the post-tribulationists holding that this translation will take place almost simultaneously with our Lord's appearance upon earth. "On the same 'day'," says one of our post-tribulation friends, "and probably only a few moments apart, He comes *for* His saints, and *with* His saints. The dead and living go up to meet Him as He descends, join His train and accompany Him back as He stands on the Mount of Olives and destroys antichrist and his armies."

This argument is based, in considerable degree, upon the assumption, by the post-tribulationists, that the terms "the day," "that day," "the last day," "the day of Christ," "the day of the Lord," "the day of the Lord Jesus," "the day of Jesus Christ," and "the day of the Lord Jesus Christ," are identical, and that these expressions refer to *one day of twenty-four hours.*

In an earlier chapter we have pointed out that there is definite, scriptural distinction between "the day of the Lord," which is synonymous with "the day of Jehovah" of the Old Testament and speaks of judgment and disaster, and "the day of Christ" (embracing also "the day of Jesus Christ," "the day of the Lord Jesus," and "the day of the Lord Jesus Christ"—all the names that the Son of God bore on earth, in His humanity), which always alludes to salvation, rejoicing, or blessing.

In regard to the assumption that these days are periods of twenty-four hours, suppose we examine a passage where "the day of the Lord" is used, namely II Peter 3:10: "But the day of the Lord will come," says the apostle, "as a thief in the night; in the which the heavens shall pass away with a great noise, and the elements shall melt with fervent heat, the earth also and the works that are therein shall be burned up." In comparing this description of events that will occur in "the day of the Lord," with those denoted in I Thessalonians 5:1–10, it is evident that there is considerable difference. The reason is that the day of the Lord extends over one thousand years. That which is predicted in I Thessalonians 5 has to do with the Lord's coming at the beginning of the Millennium, whereas that which is prophesied in II Peter 3 pertains to the end of the Millennium (cf. Rev. 20:11, 21:1). These "days" of prophecy are not confined, of necessity, to periods of twenty-four hours, but they signify spans of time when God will act in specific ways.

Returning now to the supposition of the post-tribulationists that Christ's coming *for* and *with* His saints is almost simultaneous, "probably only a few minutes apart," we affirm, entirely apart from what has been discussed in earlier studies, that such a descent leaves no interval for two events that will, according to the Scriptures, take place between the two aspects of our Lord's second coming (that is, His coming *for* His saints and *with* them), namely: the judgment seat of Christ, and the marriage supper of the Lamb.

"For we must all appear before the judgment seat of Christ; that every one may receive the things done in his body, according to that he hath done, whether it be good or bad" (II Cor. 5:10). This is written to Christians. While there is no condemnatory judgment to them which are in Christ Jesus (Rom. 8:1), every believer must give an account of himself for his life after he is saved (Rom. 14:10, 12). This will be at the judgment seat of Christ, and the result will be reward or loss of reward to every child of God (I Cor. 3: 8–15). These rewards are symbolically referred to in many instances as crowns (I Cor. 9:25; I Thess. 2:19; I Pet. 5:4; etc.).

Where and when will this judgment of believers' works take place? It will be when the Lord Jesus Christ returns to the earth at the beginning of the Millennium that the judgment of nations will occur (Matt. 25:31 ff). After the Millennium, the judgment of the great white throne will come to pass (Rev. 20:11 ff). But neither of these judgments is the judgment of the works of believers in Christ.

From II Timothy 4:8 we learn that the rewards will be presented to all of the saints at one time, and all "at that day." It will be at Christ's "appearing and His kingdom" that He will judge the living and the dead (vs. 1), the suggestion being, if we mistake not, that He will judge the spiritually living at His appearing, and the spiritually dead at His kingdom. We *do* know, however, that Christ will judge and reward His own when He comes, "at the resurrection of the just," for it is attested by several Scriptures (Matt. 16:27; Luke 14:14; I Cor. 4:5). "And, behold, I come quickly," says the glorified Christ, "and My reward is with Me, to give every man according as his work shall be" (Rev. 22:12). Furthermore, when the marriage supper of the Lamb takes place, when He takes His bride, the Church, it is said that "to her was granted that she should be arrayed in fine linen, clean and white: for the fine linen is the righteousnesses of saints" (Rev. **19:8**). Here is intimation, surely, of our Lord's acknowledgment of the "things done in the body." The judgment seat of Christ will occur when He comes, and it is evident that it will be in the air or in heaven itself, before the marriage supper of the Lamb.

The marriage supper of the Lamb will be held immediately prior to our Lord's return in power and great glory, when He rides forth from heaven as the "Faithful and True," in righteousness to judge and make war; when His armies, "clothed in fine linen, white and clean," the garments of His bride, will follow Him as He comes back to the earth to smite the nations and to tread the winepress of the fierceness and wrath of Almighty God, as King of kings and Lord of lords (Rev. **19:11–16**). Can the judgment seat of Christ in the air or in heaven, and the marriage supper of the Lamb in heaven be consummated within a few minutes? How can it be stated absolutely that the Rapture and Christ's return in power take place almost simultaneously, the saints meeting Him in the air and immediately joining His train and accompanying Him back to earth? After the raptured saints meet the Lord in the air they must receive their rewards, and they must ascend with Him to heaven to be present at the marriage supper of the Lamb. There can be no marriage supper if there is no bride.

There must be an interval of time, it would seem, for these things to be accomplished. We believe, from what we have discovered in earlier studies, that this time-period will be identical in duration with that which we know as the Tribulation. The judgment of believers' works will begin when Christ comes for His saints before the Tribulation; the marriage supper of the Lamb and His bride will be partaken of prior to Christ's advent with His saints at the end of the Tribulation.

CHAPTER X

THE HOUR OF TRIAL

In pursuance of the truth concerning the matter under discussion, our investigation brings us now to the book of The Revelation. And the first Scripture that we would examine is one that is among the golden texts of those who hold the pretribulation view in regard to the time of the Rapture, namely, Revelation 3:10, a portion of our Lord's message to the church at Philadelphia: "Because thou hast kept the word of My patience, I also will keep thee from the hour of temptation, which shall come upon all the world, to try them that dwell upon the earth."

To interpret any Scripture it is necessary to know something of the background, which may be discovered by the immediate context in which the passage under consideration is found and all that precedes it in the particular book involved. We assume that those who are following these studies have at least a working knowledge of The Revelation. However, for the sake of refreshing our memories, we shall review the first three chapters of the book in the briefest possible way.

The name of the last book of the Bible would be properly taken from the first five words, "The Revelation of Jesus Christ," rather than that which we find in most editions of the Bible, "The Revelation of St. John the Divine." This writing is the revelation of our Lord Jesus Christ, "which God gave unto Him" to show us, His servants, things which must shortly come to pass. This revelation was sent to the Apostle John, to whom it was signified, that is, *made known by signs.* The book is a book of symbols, therefore, but it is not a hidden book. It is a revelation, an unveiling. It was written to show future

things to us, but these coming events will not be revealed apart
from prayerful study and careful comparison of Scripture with
Scripture.

In chapter 1, beginning with verse 9, the apostle records a
vision which he had during his exile on the Isle of Patmos. In
this vision he had a view of the risen Christ which immediately
demonstrates the symbolic character of the book. For He
whom John saw is described as having hair like wool, eyes like
flames of fire, a mouth from which a two-edged sword pro-
truded, and feet like brass. This is not the appearance of our
blessed Lord. Reverently we say it: He is not a monstrosity.
This is figurative language, speaking of His eternal Sonship,
His discerning eyes, His speech conformed in every way to the
Word of God, and the fact that He must trample in judgment
upon His enemies. The key to this symbolism is discovered by
searching the Scriptures to find the typical meanings of the
figures here employed. For example, in Daniel 7:9, He who is
called "the Ancient of days" is said to have hair like pure wool;
and, in Hebrews 4:12, the Word of God is compared to a
sharp two-edged sword.

At the end of chapter 1 there is written a very helpful key
to the understanding of the book as a whole. It is not a man-
made key but was spoken by the Lord Himself, who told John:
"Write the things which thou hast seen, and the things which
are, and the things which shall be hereafter," or, "after these
things" (vs. 19). And then the Lord revealed the meanings of
the stars and lampstands which John saw: the seven stars are
the angels, or messengers, of the seven churches; and the seven
lampstands are the seven churches themselves. This is what
John saw. It is recorded in chapter 1, and here is the first division of the book.

The second division of the book will be found in chapters
2 and 3. Therein the apostle gives in detail our Lord's messages

from on high to seven churches that were in existence at the time that the apostle saw the vision and wrote the book.

The third division, that which pertains to "the things which shall be hereafter," or, "after these things," begins with chapter 4 and continues to the end of the book. For chapter 4 opens with these words: "After this I looked, and, behold a door was opened in heaven: and the first voice which I heard was as it were of a trumpet talking with me; which said, Come up hither, and I will show thee things which must be hereafter," or, "after these things" (vs. 1).

It is with the second division of the book, pertaining to "the things which are," that we are occupied on this occasion. This is found, as we have already stated, in Revelation 2 and 3.

There were more than seven churches in Asia when the ascended Christ sent these messages to Ephesus, Smyrna, Pergamos, Thyatira, Sardis, Philadelphia, and Laodicea. Seven is the number of completeness, and the choice of seven churches suggests that the messages to them were to all the churches in Asia, as indeed they were. The commendations, warnings, and exhortations in them are for individuals also, as is evidenced by the recurring expression: "He that hath an ear to hear, let him hear what the Spirit saith unto the churches." Further, it seems apparent that, since this is a portion of God's Word, these messages are for all churches throughout the full Church age; for the circumstances and characteristics that are manifest in the designated churches of Revelation 2 and 3 are equally conspicuous today in assemblies on every side. Finally, we have here a prophetic view of church history. Without going into a detailed study of the subject, it is plain that we are able to see now, as we look back through the centuries, the nature and marks of the professing church from apostolic times until the present hour, and beyond: there is Ephesus, the first-love church with its decline; Smyrna, the suffering church under Roman persecutions; Pergamos, the worldly church that issued at the so-called conversion of Constantine; Thyatira, when Rome was at its greatest power; Sardis, the Reformation church; Philadelphia, the church that returned to the Word of God and found the open door to missionary ministry; and Laodicea, the apostate church of the last days of the age.

It is in the message to the church at Philadelphia, the church that has kept Christ's Word and has not denied His name, that our text appears, and we quote it again: "Because thou has kept the word of My patience, I will also keep thee from the hour of temptation, which shall come upon all the world, to try them that dwell upon the earth" (Rev. 3:10). The expression that will receive our initial attention is this: "I will keep thee from the hour of temptation [or *trial,* or *tribulation*], which is to come upon all the world."

It is very clear that to this church and to those that have ears to hear (vs. 13), our Lord gives the promise that He will keep them from the hour of tribulation that the whole world will experience, which must quite obviously be the Tribulation referred to in Daniel 12, Matthew 24, and Revelation 5-19. Post- and pre-tribulationists are generally agreed upon this point. Why, then, is there any question about whether or not the Church will be translated before the Tribulation? It is because there is disagreement as to whether the word "from" denotes "through" or "out of." Our post-tribulation brethren hold and affirm that our Lord Jesus Christ will keep His own *safely through* the Tribulation, as the Lord kept Israel through the plagues that fell upon Egypt and as He guarded Noah safely through the judgment of the flood. Pre-tribulationists believe and teach that our Lord will take His own *out of* the world before the Tribulation sets in, as Enoch was translated before the flood.

The word rendered "from" is from the Greek preposition *ek.* It has various connotations that denote *exit out of* or *separation from* something with which there has been connection: from a place, from the midst of a group, from a condition or state, etc. The preposition is used twice in John 17:15, once denoting *out of,* and once, *from* (while still, as it were, in the presence of): "I pray not," our Lord says to the Father in His intercessory prayer, "that Thou shouldest take them *out of* [*ek*] the world, but that Thou shouldest keep them *from* [*ek*] evil." Thus it may be seen that the post-tribulationists have a point of argument for their view of Revelation 3:10. Having said this much, however, suppose we examine more fully the preposition, the text, and the context.

Regarding the preposition *ek,* which is used over 800 times in the New Testament, only once can we find an instance where it is actually rendered "through"; that is in Galatians 3:8, "through faith," where the obvious sense is "by."

Ek is rendered "out of" hundreds of times, as for example: "*Out of* Egypt have I called My Son" (Matt. 2:15); "First cast out the beam *out of* thine own eye" (Matt. 7:5); "For *out of* the heart proceed evil thoughts" (Matt. 15:19); "And [many bodies of the saints] came *out of* the graves after His resurrection" (Matt. 27:53); "I will not blot out his name *out of* the book of life" (Rev. 3:5); "I will spue thee *out of* My mouth" (Rev. 3:16).

Again, we have traced the preposition *ek,* when translated "from," 150 times in the New Testament, to find no more than five occasions when it could possibly denote "through" or "in," and only in one instance, its second use in John 17:15 to which we have already alluded, in the exact sense that the post-tributionists suggest for Revelation 3:10. The usual Greek for "through" is *dia,* and for "in," *en, eis, epi,* and *kata.* It would seem that, if the Spirit of God intended to convey to the readers of this passage that the Lord would keep His own *through* or *in* the hour of trial, He would have used *dia,* or *eis,* or *epi* or *kata* and not *ek,* which surely implies *out of* rather than *through* or *in.*

It is well to observe the text itself. Those to whom the Lord is speaking are said to have kept "the word of My patience," an expression that suggests, at least, patient waiting *for Him*. "And the Lord direct your hearts into the love of God, and into the patient waiting for Christ" (II Thess. 3:5). "For we know that the whole creation groaneth and travaileth in pain together until now. And not only they, but ourselves also, which have the firstfruits of the Spirit, even we ourselves groan within ourselves, waiting for the adoption, to wit, the redemption of our body. . . . But if we hope for that we see not, then do we with patience wait for it" (Rom. 8:22-25). The redemption of the body will be at His coming, and we who wait for Him are keeping the word of His patience.

It is important to note that it is not simply temptation, or tribulation, that our Lord promises to keep His own from, but it is *"the hour of* temptation, which is to come upon all the world."* While it may be proposed that the Lord can keep His own *from trial* simply by keeping them *safely through* it, it does not seem to us that this can be stated with equal force in regard to *the hour* of temptation that the whole world will experience. The *hour* itself must be lived through by all who are in the world contemporaneous with it, and the only way that one can be kept *from* that *hour* is to be taken *out of* the world when the hour strikes.

Again, examine the last clause of our text: "to try them that dwell upon the earth." Those who are to undergo this tribulation, "them that dwell upon the earth," comprise a class of people that is referred to in such a way or by kindred expressions throughout the book (6:10; 8:13; 11:10; 12:12; 13:8, 12, 14; 14:6; 17:2, 8), a faction that is entirely earthly in its thinking and in no way whatever a heavenly people. There is not the slightest suggestion that the Lord's blood-purchased Church must remain here for that experience, even as a protected spectator.

Finally, the context suggests that Christ's keeping of those who have kept the word of His patience *"from* the hour of temptation,"* will be *out of* it, called upward by His rapture-shout; for the following verse declares: "Behold, I come quickly: hold that fast which thou hast, that no man take thy crown." Such a crown will be a form of reward, and when our Lord comes, He will reward His own. Almost His last message from heaven was this: "Behold, I come quickly; and My reward is with Me; to give every man according as his work shall be" (Rev. 22:12).

So, while the word rendered "from" in Revelation 3:10 may lexically denote "through," the weight of evidence implies quite the contrary: that the Lord Jesus Christ will keep His Church *"out of* the hour of trial which shall come upon all the world, to try them that dwell upon the earth." Far from reading this into the Scriptures, as some of our post-tribulation brethren accuse us of doing, it impresses us that the more thoroughly this Scripture is examined, the more completely the pre-tribulation rapture of the Church is established and confirmed in it.

CHAPTER XI

THE FOUR AND TWENTY ELDERS

The history of the church is foretold in Revelation 2 and 3, as we pointed out in the previous chapter. Following this record of the church's activity, a new division of The Revelation, the third section of the book, is introduced with the first verse of chapter 4: "After this I looked," says John, "and, behold, a door was opened in heaven: and the first voice which I heard was as it were of a trumpet talking with me; which said, Come up hither, and I will show thee things which must be hereafter," or, "after these things."

The Church age is now past in this vision. What the apostle sees includes an immediate scene in heaven, in chapters 4 and 5, and later scenes affecting both heaven and earth, inaugurated by the breaking of seals and the riding forth of the four horsemen of chapter 6. Chapters 4 and 5 seem clearly to describe an interlude, as it were, just prior to the amazing events that accompany the breaking of the seals, the sounding of trumpets, and the pouring of vials in judgment—the Tribulation that is to come upon this earth.

John heard the voice, which said: "Come up hither." And we read: "And immediately I was in the spirit; and, behold, a throne was set in heaven, and one sat on the throne. And He that sat was to look upon like a jasper and a sardine stone: and there was a rainbow round about the throne, in sight like unto an emerald. And round about the throne were four and twenty seats [lit., *thrones*]: and upon the seats [thrones] I saw four and twenty elders sitting, clothed in white raiment; and they had on their heads crowns of gold. And out of the throne proceeded lightnings and thunderings and voices . . . (Rev. 4:2–5).

The question immediately arises: Who are the four and twenty elders spoken of here? There is diversity of opinion regarding their identity. Some would have us believe that the elders represent the overcomers mentioned in Revelation 2 and 3. Others identify them as the principalities and powers of Ephesians 1:21 and Colossians 1:16. Still others state that they are the angels and authorities of I Peter 3:22. Some of our post-tribulation brethren dismiss them as being incapable of identification; the twenty-four elders are heavenly beings, they say, a sort of senior officialdom of celestial beings. One of the most ardent of the post-tribulation writers states that the elders "are glorious heavenly beings taking the lead in the praise and worship of God," and declares: "There is absolutely no evidence that these twenty-four elders are human beings at all, or have any connection with the redeemed." We disagree with this brother and others who identify the four and twenty elders as celestial beings rather than redeemed members of the human race. In fact, if we can show from Scripture that the twenty-four elders symbolically represent redeemed humanity, the case of the post-tribulationists is considerably weakened.

The Revelation is a book of symbols. Much of one's understanding of the book comes from searching out, in other Scriptures, the meaning of the figurative language of The Apocalypse. There is not one place in the Bible where angelic beings are referred to as "elders," but there are many instances of men being thus designated (Gen. 50:7; Ex. 3:16; Lev. 4:15; Num. 11:16; Deut. 5:23; Psa. 107:32; Isa. 37:2; Eze. 8:1; Matt. 15:2; Luke 7:3; Acts 4:5; I Tim. 5:17; Heb. 11:2; I Pet. 5:1). The word, "elders," is used twelve times in The Revelation and, by context, the elders are always distinguished from celestial beings. Never, prior to the occasion described in Revelation 4, do we see elders in heaven but always on earth.

John was not the only one of God's servants to view heavenly scenes.

Isaiah, in the year that king Uzziah died, "saw also the Lord sitting upon a throne, high and lifted up" (Isa. 6:1). The ancient seer observed many wonders in this vision, and he saw the seraphim, angelic beings who cried one to another: "Holy, holy, holy, is the Lord of hosts: the whole earth is full of His glory." But Isaiah saw no four and twenty elders sitting upon four and twenty thrones.

Ezekiel, the son of Buzi, by the river Chebar in the land of the Chaldeans, had a vision in which he saw "the appearance of the likeness of the glory of the Lord" (Eze. 1:3, 28). In that experience the ancient prophet beheld many marvelous things, and he saw four living creatures, celestial beings whom John gazed upon centuries later. But Ezekiel did not look upon four and twenty thrones occupied by a like number of elders.

Prior to the occasion when the Apostle John heard the voice, as it were a trumpet, which said: "Come up hither," he, too, had a vision, on the isle of Patmos, when he looked into the glory to behold astonishing things. But he saw no such thrones and elders as he later beheld.

Why did Isaiah, who viewed other wonders of heaven, who looked upon the seraphim, fail to see the elders? Why did Ezekiel, who beheld other marvels—the precious, colorful stones, the rainbow, the glories, who viewed the four living creatures, miss the four and twenty elders seated upon thrones? Why did not John, in his former vision, take note of their presence in heaven? These servants of God did not see or describe the four and twenty thrones, and the four and twenty elders seated upon them, because the elders were not yet in heaven. It was when John was caught up into heaven in an experience somewhat symbolic of the coming translation of the Church, that the four and twenty elders are first seen enthroned about the throne of the Lord. Here is a new body in heaven, at the end of the Church age and prior to the Tribulation. They are not angels. They are not the seraphim. They are not the cherubim. They are not the four living creatures. They are evidently human beings, redeemed saints, as further examination of the passage will confirm.

We find that these elders are said to be clothed in white raiment. We are reminded at once of the bridal garment of the Lamb's wife, "fine linen, clean and white" (Rev. 19:8), which speaks of the righteousnesses of the saints; and again, of the clothing of the armies that will march forth with Him who is called "Faithful and True, The Word of God, King of kings, and Lord of lords"—"fine linen, white and clean" (Rev. 19:14). White raiment is a symbol of righteousness; in the case of redeemed humanity, it is used in contrast with the filthy rags of human righteousness (Isa. 64:6). For in the precious blood of Christ the filthy rags of sin are made clean, as white as snow.

It may be proposed that angels, too, have been described as garbed in white raiment, as, for example, the two men in white apparel who prophesied to our Lord's disciples as to His coming again in like manner as they had seen Him go into heaven (Acts 1:10). But we have observed that elders are not angels.

Furthermore, these four and twenty elders are described as having crowns of gold upon their heads. There are two Greek words for "crown"—*diadema,* the monarch's crown; and *stephanos,* the victor's wreath. The word *diadema* is used only thrice in the New Testament. In each instance it has reference to the crowning of either a supernatural being or to one who is supernaturally inspired for a particular task. The former designation is employed in Revelation 12:3, where the dragon (Satan) is said to bear "seven crowns," and in chapter 19:12, where the Lord Jesus Christ is seen coming as "King of kings." The third time that *diadema* is used is in connection with the "beast . . . out of the sea" (Rev. 13:1).

The crowns that the elders wear are *stephanoi.* Do we ever

read of the angels reigning or wearing crowns? No; but those who participate in the first resurrection are to reign with Christ (Rev. **20**:6). And to whom are crowns given but to believers in Christ? "Henceforth," says Paul, "there is laid up for me a crown [*stephanos*] of righteousness, which the Lord, the righteous judge, shall give me at that day: and not to me only, but unto all them also that love His appearing" (II Tim. **4**:8). It is the *stephanos* that is referred to also by James and Peter when they speak of the crowns of life and of glory (Jas. **1**:12; I Pet. **5**:4). Only Christ's blood-purchased saints are promised such crowns. They are His rewards, given in grace. They are to be given all at one time, and all "at that day." What day? When He comes. "Behold, I come quickly; and My reward is with Me, to give every man according as His work shall be" (Rev. **22**:12). Since crowns are for the redeemed, since the elders wear crowns, since those crowns will be given to all at one time, "at that day," and since, when our Lord comes His reward is with Him, it seems evident that He will have come for His own when that which is described in Revelation **4** takes place.

Elders are representatives of the people. Thus the seventy elders bore with Moses the burden of the people of Israel (Num. **11**:16, 17). As for the number twenty-four, it is twice twelve, a biblical number of administration, and may signify here the saints of both the Old and New Testaments. Such a correspondence between the redeemed people of God is seen again in this same book wherein, in the description of the New Jerusalem, it is written that the twelve gates of the city will bear the names of the twelve tribes of Israel, and that the twelve foundation stones of the wall of the city will carry the names of the twelve apostles. Certainly the identification of the four and twenty elders as representatives of all the redeemed— raptured, clothed in the righteousness of God in Christ, crowned with victor's wreaths, enthroned in the presence of the throne of the Lord—has more evidence to substantiate it than to call them angels or celestial beings of another order.

Nor have we yet finished with this identification. For we find these elders falling down to worship Him that is seated upon the throne in heaven, and casting their crowns before Him, saying: "Thou art worthy, O Lord, to receive glory and honor and power; for Thou hast created all things, and for Thy pleasure they are and were created" (Rev. 4:10, 11). There appears to be only one reason why these elders should choose this particular time to cast their crowns at the feet of the Lord. It is because they have just received them! We do not know that any angel was ever crowned; but if one were, he would surely not select this moment to lay his crown at the feet of the Lord; he would do it when he received the crown. For the Lord alone is worthy of glory and honor and power. Thus, this very act of casting crowns at His feet suggests that the crowns have only just been received; and the only future award of crowns that Scripture describes is the rewarding of Christ's own at His coming.

Finally, we read of the new song that is sung by the four and twenty elders: "Thou art worthy to take the book, and to open the seals thereof: for Thou wast slain, and hast redeemed *us* to God by Thy blood out of every kindred, and tongue, and people, and nation; hast made *us* unto our God kings and priests: and *we* shall reign on the earth" (Rev. 5:9, 10). Here is a song sung to the Lamb. Purposely we have quoted the verse as it is written in the Authorized Version, quite aware of the fact that the pronouns, which we have italicized, are not in the Greek text. Later translations supply the words "men," or "them," in place of "us," and still other versions omit any nouns or pronouns.

The fact that the first person—that is, "we" and "us,"—is not indicated in the Greek is supposed, by some, to spell defeat to the pre-tribulation position. But it does nothing of the kind.

First of all, there is clear intimation that the four living creatures unite with the four and twenty elders in singing this new song. But they could never say to the Lord Jesus Christ: "Thou hast redeemed *us* by Thy blood out of every kindred, and tongue, and people, and nation"!

Furthermore, the fact that no pronouns are found in some of the Greek texts does not deprive the twenty-four elders of including themselves within the blessings of the song. A very apt illustration of this fact will be found in Exodus 15, where there is recorded the song of the redeemed Israelites. "Then sang Moses and the children of Israel this song unto the Lord. . . . Thou in Thy mercy hast led forth *the people* which Thou hast redeemed: Thou hast guided *them* in Thy strength unto Thy holy habitation. . . . Thou shalt bring *them* in, and plant *them* in the mountain of Thine inheritance . . ." (vss. 1, 13, 17). Would anyone claim that, because the first person is not used in the pronouns in this song, Moses and the Israelites were not singing of themselves? Surely not! And so the new song of Revelation 5, sung by the elders, proclaims the worthiness of the Lamb slain for them, of Him who redeemed them, and us too, out of every kindred, and tongue, and people, and nation, by His blood.

That the four and twenty elders of Revelation 4 and 5 designate the raptured saints of the Old and New Testaments is suggested by fact after fact. No other interpretation falls so in line with Scripture as a whole. These elders represent all the redeemed of God, from creation to the end of the Church age, translated into heaven, enthroned, clothed, and crowned in the presence of the Lord *before* the awful judgments of the Tribulation begin.

CHAPTER XII

THE SAINTS AND THE SERVANTS OF GOD

If it be true that the Church is to be translated before the Tribulation begins and that, as we endeavored to show in the preceding chapter, the four and twenty elders of Revelation 4 and 5 represent the saints of Old Testament times and this present dispensation, seated about the throne in heaven prior to the breaking of the seals that inaugurate the Tribulation, the question arises as to who they are who are designated frequently, in later chapters of The Revelation, as "the saints" (8:3, 4; 11:18; 13:7, 10; 14:12; 15:3; 16:6; 17:6; 18:24; 19:8; 20:9) and "the servants of God" (7:3; 10:7; 11:18; 19:2, 5; 22:3, 6). For if our premise be correct concerning the time of the Rapture, the saints and servants of God mentioned in later chapters of The Revelation cannot represent the Church unless these saints be shown to be in heaven during this period. Equally true it is that, if those designated as "the saints" or "the servants of God" can be proved to be the Church on earth during the Tribulation, the Church must go through some portion of the Tribulation.

It is not sufficient for us to point out that the words "church" and "churches" do not appear in The Revelation after chapter 3:14 and 22 respectively, except in chapter 22:16, where the ascended Christ states, at the conclusion of this book of prophecy, that He has sent His messenger to testify of the things written in the book, "in the churches"; that is, He is sending the message of The Revelation to the churches that are on earth at this present time, in the Church age, as indicated at the beginning of the book (1:1, 4; 2:1; etc.). The

Church is designated in Scripture, however, apart from the use of the word itself. In fact, throughout the New Testament, members of the mystical body of Christ are referred to as "the saints" equally as frequently as the body itself is called "the Church." Thus, even though the word "church" is not found anywhere from chapters 6–19 in The Revelation, the designation, "the saints," is written twelve times, and "the servants of God" are mentioned seven times. It must be borne in mind also that the terms, "the saints" and "the servants of God," are not confined to the Church of God. His people were called "the saints" in Old Testament times, before the Church began (Psa. 97:10; Prov. 2:8), and were referred to as His "servants" as well (Ezra 5:11; Psa. 34:22), so that these designations, when found in Bible prophecies concerning the Tribulation, do not automatically identify those of whom they speak as the Church.

In connection with our present purpose, we can eliminate entirely any consideration of these classifications of God's people when they are seen to be in heaven; for the inquiry that we are pursuing is to discover whether the Scriptures teach that the Church is on earth during the Tribulation. Consequently we shall not discuss Revelation 15:3 (where, actually, the word "saints" is erroneous; it should be "ages"); 19:8; and 20:9 (which, without contradiction, has to do with the end of the Millennium). As far as the other allusions to the two expressions are concerned, we can learn the answer to the problem as a whole by examining certain key passages, Scriptures which those who oppose the doctrine of the pre-tribulation rapture of the Church cite to prove their viewpoint.

The first reference to the servants of God on earth, after the breaking of the seals of Revelation 6, is found in chapter 7. There we read of the message of the angel of the living God, who orders the four angels of verse 1 to withhold for a time their destructive plagues, saying: "Hurt not the earth, neither the sea, nor the trees, till we have sealed the servants of our God in their foreheads" (vs. 3).

Who are these servants of God? Do they compose the Church? The Church has already been sealed by the Holy Spirit until the day of redemption (Eph. 4:30), so that we should not expect that its members would need to be sealed again. However, we are not left to conjecture on this point, for the sealed servants are identified: "an hundred and forty and four thousand of all the tribes of the children of Israel" (vs. 4), and they are called by tribal names, 12,000 of each tribe. This is not the Church. Members of Christ's body, the Church, are not called "the children of Israel."* You Gentiles, who have been born again through faith in Christ, of what tribe are you? You are not of Israel but of Christ. The 144,000 sealed servants of God are Jews.

In the same chapter we see "a great multitude, which no man could number, of all nations, and kindreds, and people, and tongues," standing before the throne (vs. 9). Do these compose the Church? Some propose that they do. Yet they are described in this wise in the Scriptures: "These are they which came out of great tribulation, and have washed their robes, and made them white in the blood of the Lamb" (vs. 14). The scene appears to be on earth, according to the divine provision for them that is described in verses 15–17, which suggests that it occurs at the beginning of the Millennium, when multitudes of the Gentiles will be brought over to enter into millennial blessing, like the sheep of Matthew 25:31, 32.

It is immaterial for our purpose whether the figure of 144,-000 be taken literally or symbolically. It represents, in either event, a remnant of the Jews who will be saved during the Tribulation. That they will be born anew during the time of

---

* It is quite true that all men and women of faith are said to be children of Abraham, "who is the father of us all" (Rom. 4:16), but that is quite different from the designation "children of Israel."

Jacob's trouble is predicted more than once in the Old Testament. We cite two passages only: "And they that be wise [of the children of Israel at the time of the Tribulation] shall shine as the brightness of the firmament; and they that turn many to righteousness as the stars for ever and ever" (Dan. 12:3); and, "Who has heard such a thing? Who hath seen such things? Shall the earth be made to bring forth in one day? Or shall a nation be born at once? For as soon as Zion travailed, she brought forth her children . . . For I know their works and their thoughts: it shall come that I will gather all nations and tongues; and they shall come, and see My glory" (Isa. 66:8, 18; see also Hos. 6:1, Mic. 5:3; Zech. 12:10).

Evidently the Spirit of God will be poured out upon Israel in that day. Many of that nation will turn to the Lord; and many from among the Gentiles, seeing the glory of God in His people, Israel, will also turn to the Lord. It is not amiss, therefore, for us to infer that the 144,000 will be the publishers or evangelists of the Gospel of the kingdom to the whole world in that day (cf. Matt. 24:14).

Those who oppose the position of the pre-tribulationists submit that we are fanciful in understanding the Scriptures thus. One of the chief proponents of post-tribulationism endeavors so energetically to disprove that the 144,000 compose a remnant of the nation Israel saved during the Tribulation, and the great multitude, out of all Gentile nations, the converts of these Israelites, that he makes this statement concerning our position: it is an unscriptural innovation, in which we would proclaim "the prodigious missionary tour of the world in 1,260 days by an army of half-converted Jews, still in their sins. Preachers without life," he continues, "without forgiveness, and without the Holy Ghost in the soul, will do in 1,260 days what the whole Christian Church has been unable to do in 1,900 years—evangelize the world, and convert the 'overwhelming majority' of the inhabitants of the world to God."

We cite the above quotation from our brother's writings in order to show how utterly illogical and unreliable such reasoning is. It the pre-tribulationist fanciful? He is less so than is the aforementioned writer in making such a statement. What, may we ask, is a half-converted Jew? A man is either born again or not born again. There is no such thing as half-conversion. What pre-tribulationist *ever* spoke of the 144,000 as being "without life, without forgiveness, and without the Holy Ghost in the soul"? It is quite true that we have stated that the Holy Spirit, as the constant indweller of the believer, is to be taken out of the way at the time of the Rapture, basing this doctrine upon II Thessalonians 2:7; but we do not know how He will act upon or within the saved of the tribulation period. Of course, neither pre- nor post-tribulationist is able to say with authority whether "a great multitude, which no man could number, of all nations, and kindreds, and people, and tongues" will or will not constitute "the 'overwhelming majority' of the inhabitants of the world."

We affirm, however, that it is less fanciful to hold that the 144,000 compose a remnant of Israel, and that the great multitude from the nations are their converts during the Tribulation, when backed up by the Scriptures alluded to, than to suggest that either the band of 144,000 from the tribes of Israel or the great multitude of Gentiles is the Church still here on earth during the Tribulation. The throne of God will not be on the earth during the Tribulation, neither will God have an earthly temple in which His servants will serve Him day and night during the Tribulation, nor will the Lamb, our Lord Jesus Christ, be in the midst of God's throne on earth during the Tribulation.

Another Scripture, to which the post-tribulationists would have us give answer, if we would prove that the Church will not be left on earth during the Tribulation, is Revelation 10:7: "But in the days of the voice of the seventh angel, when he shall begin to sound, the mystery of God should be finished, as He hath declared to His servants the prophets." The problem here is not the allusion to "His servants the prophets," for it is agreed almost universally among students of the Bible that this description applies here to the divinely inspired human instruments who penned the Scriptures. The issue has to do, rather, with the fact that it will be in the days of the voice of the seventh angel that, we are told, "the mystery of God should be finished."

Frankly, we see no problem here at all. It would never have occurred to us that this verse could be related to the Church unless our attention had been called especially to it by a beloved brother who teaches a post-tribulation Rapture. If the Scripture stated that, "in the days of the voice of the seventh angel, when he shall begin to sound, *the mystery of Christ and His Church* should be finished, as He hath declared to His servants the prophets," we would admit that those who allege that the Church will be on earth for a portion or all of the Tribulation would have a strong point. However, that is not what the Scripture tells us. It is not "the mystery of Christ and His Church" that is to be finished at the sounding of the voice of the seventh angel, but "the mystery of God." These are not identical.

The New Testament discloses a number of mysteries: the mysteries of the kingdom of the heavens (Matt. 13): the mystery that blindness in part has happened to Israel (Rom. 11:25); the mystery that we shall not all sleep but that we shall all be changed (I Cor. 15:51–53); the mystery of lawlessness (II Thess. 2:7); etc. Among these mysteries—truths previously hidden but revealed in certain Scriptures—are these two: (1) Christ and His Church (as to the fact that Jews and Gentiles are fellow-heirs with Christ and of one body, the Church, in Eph. 3:3–11; and concerning the Church as the bride of Christ, in Eph. 5:25–32); and (2) the mystery of God and of Christ (Col. 2:2, 3; cf. I Cor. 2:7). It is this latter mystery that is to be finished when the seventh angel sounds.

What is "the mystery of God"? According to Colossians 2:2, 3, "the mystery of God and Christ" is that all the treasures of wisdom and knowledge are hid in our Lord. There has always, since the first rebellion, been the mystery of God as to why He permits evil, why He does not act to overthrow Satan and His enemies, etc. This mystery is answered in Christ, "in whom dwelleth all the fulness of the Godhead bodily" (Col. 2:9), and it will be finished, completed, no longer a mystery, "in the days of the voice of the seventh angel."

An examination of the first portion of Revelation 10 will bring to light who this angel is—a "mighty angel . . . clothed with a cloud . . . a rainbow upon His head . . . His face as it were the sun . . . His feet as pillars of fire." It is the Lord Jesus Christ, the Son of God. He is seen to come out of heaven and to give certain instructions to the ancient seer, John, concerning prophecy, and to reveal further things pertaining to the end time. This precedes the sounding of the seventh trumpet when, at last, the kingdoms of this world will become the kingdom of Christ, who will judge, and recompense, and reign forever. Thus "the mystery of God," which has perplexed mankind for so long, will be finished. Evil will be judged and righteousness will prevail in Christ, "in whom dwelleth all the fulness of the Godhead bodily."

The completion of the mystery of God has naught to do with the Church. The Church, which is the body and bride of Christ, will be completed when the last member is added to it and it is caught up to be with the Lord at the sound of the glad rapture-shout. This will be, we believe, before the first seal of Revelation 6 is broken, before any portion of the Tribulation sets in.

CHAPTER XIII

THE LAST TRUMP AND THE
SEVENTH TRUMPET

The final key verse of The Revelation, in which **God's peo-**
ple who will be on earth during the Tribulation are referred to
as "Thy servants the prophets, and . . . the saints," is chapter
11:18. It will be profitable to quote quite a long passage in
connection with our examination of this portion of prophecy.

"And the seventh angel sounded; and there were great
voices in heaven, saying, The kingdoms of this world are become the kingdom of our Lord, and of His Christ; and He
shall reign for ever and ever. And the four and twenty elders,
which sat before God on their thrones, fell upon their faces,
and worshipped God, saying, We give Thee thanks, O Lord
God Almighty, which art, and wast: because Thou hast taken
to Thee Thy great power, and hast reigned. And the nations
were angry, and Thy wrath is come, and the time of the dead,
that they should be judged, and that Thou shouldest give reward unto Thy servants the prophets, and to the saints, and
them that fear Thy name, small and great; and shouldest
destroy them which destroy the earth" (Rev. **11:15–18**). Observe, please, three changes in this text from the Authorized
Version: (1) in verse 15, the italicized words *"the kingdoms"*
has been rendered "the kingdom," for the kingdoms of this
world will become one kingdom, the kingdom of Christ; (2)
in verse 16, the word "seats" has been changed to the proper
translation, "thrones," as also in 4:4; and (3) in verse 17, the
clause, "and art to come," has been omitted since it is an inter-
polation. The Lord is seen in this portion of The Revelation

as *now coming* and, therefore, He cannot be referred to here as the One who is to come.

Revelation 11 is an important chapter to examine in a study of the time of the Rapture in respect to the Tribulation, for upon this chapter stand or fall, in great extent, the positions of both the mid-tribulationists and the post-tribulationists. Here we have the sounding of a trumpet, resurrection, ascension of living saints, reward to God's people, and the judgment of the wicked dead. The mid-tribulationist contends that the sounding of the seventh trumpet is midway through the Tribulation and, therefore, the Rapture will take place at that time. The post-tribulationist affirms that the activities of this chapter are coincidental with that which is described in chapters 19:11–20:6 and proposes, consequently, that the Rapture will occur at the end of the Tribulation. Both schools of thought agree in identifying "the seventh trumpet" of this chapter with "the last trump" of I Corinthians 15:52 and, therefore, with "the trump of God" of I Thessalonians 4:16.

Let us ask ourselves, first of all, whether "the seventh trumpet" and "the last trump" are necessarily identical. Assuredly the seventh trumpet is the last in a series of seven soundings of trumpets. It is also the last judgment trumpet. But is it "the last trump" of I Corinthians 15:52?

It is said of the seven trumpets of The Revelation that they were given to seven angels who stood before God, in John's vision (Rev. 8:2), and that each of the seven trumpets was sounded by an angel. It is stated concerning the last trump that it "shall sound, and the dead shall be raised incorruptible, and we shall be changed" (I Cor. 15:52). That "the last trump" is "the trump of God" of I Thessalonians 4:16 is indisputable, but in neither passage is it implied that it will be sounded by an angel, although it *may* be that it will. While each of the seven trumpets of The Revelation, sounded by an angel of God, may be *a* trump of God, this fact does not automatically, establish that the seventh trumpet is *the* trump of God. The seventh trumpet introduces the final of a series of judgments; the last trump is a call to blessing untold.

The pre-tribulationist, who believes that there will be an interval of time between the sounding of the last trump and the seventh trumpet, is asked: "How can you possibly contend that the last trump will sound prior to the seventh trumpet? If any other trumpets sound after it, how can it be called 'the last trump'?" The answer is that the last trump is to be sounded for the saints whereas the seventh trumpet is to be sounded in judgment. Each is the last in its own sphere but this does not require that the two be identical.

Human illustrations are at best superficial and unsatisfactory, yet we offer one that may be of help in this instance. Some years ago the author directed a Bible conference at sea, a ten-day voyage to Bermuda and Nova Scotia, known as "The Revelation Cruise." The ship, the "S.S. Transylvania," was chartered exclusively for this cruise, since there were nearly 600 people who took the trip, almost a capacity crowd. As the hour of sailing approached, a gong was sounded and visitors to the ship were told that they must go ashore. Some departed and some did not. Five minutes before sailing time a bugle was blown and the ship's stewards on the various decks shouted: "Last bugle!" Although it was the first time that the bugle was sounded, it was the last bugle that visitors would hear, the last bugle before the ship should sail.

After the "Transylvania" had cast off from the dock, the bugle sounded again. First, it sounded for the luncheon call; then it sounded in the afternoon, preparatory to the whistle-signal for life-boat drill; the bugle sounded still again at dinner time; and the last bugle that day sounded to call passengers to the evening meeting. The last bugle for visitors was not identical with the fourth, or last, bugle for passengers. One was not confused with the other. Neither ought the last trump for the saints be confused with the last trumpet of judgment.

The significance of the term, "the last trump," in I Corinthians 15:52, inasmuch as this sounding is not one of a series of trumpetings, may possibly be that of a rallying call, or an alarm. In Numbers 10 we read of the sounding of trumpets for calling an assembly of the people and for their journeyings. There were specific calls for each of the camps of the Israelites and special calls for the whole congregation. In connection with this, Dr. Carl Armerding has an interesting comment: "The *last trump* would signify that the whole congregation was finally on the move. In a way this may illustrate what we find in I Corinthians 15:23, 'Every man in his own order [or rank —*tagmati*]: Christ the firstfruits; afterward they that are Christ's at His coming.' These last are certainly divided into at least two groups: those who have 'fallen asleep,' and those 'who are alive and remain.' . . .

" 'In a moment" and 'in the twinkling of an eye' are expressions," continues Dr. Armerding, "which are used the world around to indicate suddenness and rapidity. The fact that the third phrase, 'at the last trump,' is so closely associated with them would lead us to believe that it should be understood in the same way. If so, it will be in the nature of an *alarm,* which is the very word used in Numbers 10:5, 6 in connection with the 'journeying of the camps.' The quickening and assembling already accomplished [the former by the voice of the Lord, and the latter by the voice of the archangel— I Thess. 4:16], . . there is only one more thing necessary to set all in motion. It is 'the last trump.' That will be the final note struck on that momentous occasion."*

We shall be accused, no doubt, of straining very hard to

---

* *The Last Trump and the Seventh Trumpet,* by Carl Armerding (Loizeaux Bros., New York), reprinted from an article that appeared in *Our Hope,* December, 1942.

make the Scriptures suit our own purpose in this matter. Such
a charge is not warranted, however. For, as we shall seek to
show, the events that accompany the blowing of the seventh
trumpet cannot possibly be identified with those that accompany the last trump, the trump of God. And since this is the
case, we have endeavored to discover and set forth in these
paragraphs the way in which the expression, "the last trump,"
is employed.

We have already remarked upon the fact that, in Revelation
11, there are events such as those that are associated with the
Rapture—a trumpet sound, resurrection of the dead, ascension
of the living, and reward to God's people. Similarity, however,
does not necessarily prove identification. There is resurrection
in this chapter, that of the two witnesses (vs. 11). There is also
translation, for it is said that "they [the two witnesses] ascended
up to heaven in a cloud" (vs. 12). If two be the number of
testimony, these witnesses thus representing a multitude of
God's witness-bearing people, their resurrection and ascension
may be compared with the dead in Christ who will rise
(I Thess. 4:16); but their ascension into heaven surely cannot
be identified with those who are to be caught up, who are described as being alive and remaining at the time of Christ's
coming for His own (I Thess. 4:17). Those who have died
and have been raised do not coincide with those who are alive
and remain!

Again, the passage in The Revelation speaks of a great
earthquake, of thousands who are slain, and of the remnant
being affrighted at this time. There is nothing of this nature
in Paul's writings about the Rapture which, in his language,
is a time of blessing and comfort to all God's people.

Still further, it is to be observed that the resurrection in
Revelation 11 *precedes* the sounding of the seventh trumpet;
it does not follow the trumpet blast as it does in I Corinthians
15 and I Thessalonians 4. Some will argue: "I Corinthians

15:52 says *at* the last trump' and not *after'* it." That is so in the Authorized Version. But in the Greek the preposition is *en,* signifying *in, within, in the presence of,* etc., which assuredly is more suggestive of *after* or *coincident with* than it is of *before.*

Finally, the reference to reward (vs. 18) is said to indicate that it is the Rapture that is alluded to here. While it is true that members of Christ's body, the Church, will all be rewarded "at that day" (II Tim. 4:8), the day of His coming, it is obvious that, if the Tribulation saints are not of the redeemed family of God until after the Rapture, their rewards must be given at another time, doubtless when the Tribulation is over. It is not stated concerning the reward of Revelation 11 that it will be given in the air where the Church will receive reward but, rather, it is clearly implied that it is on the earth, just as the destruction of them that destroy the earth, in this passage, appears to be an earthly judgment. The mention of rewards for the Tribulation saints, therefore, does not pose a grave problem.

It may very well be that the events of chapter 11:15–18 take us as far, chronologically, as chapters 19:11–20:6, chapters 11:19–19:10 going back and giving a detailed description of the actors and episodes that lead up to the sounding of the seventh trumpet, just as Genesis 2 enlarges upon the concise statement of Genesis 1:26, 27 as to man's creation. The ancient seer views, with inspired eye, the return of the Lord in power and great glory, in 11:15–18, when in final wrath He comes and the kingdoms of the world become His kingdom. He rewards His servants and saints of the Tribulation period, who will reign with Him; and He destroys His enemies on the earth. And John, counting time with the divine measure which sees things of the future as already accomplished, speaks of the time having come when the dead should be judged, although that event is still actually 1,000 years distant (cf. 20:5; 11–15).

Howbeit, whether it is held that the sounding of the seventh trumpet introduces the last half of the Tribulation, that is, the Great Tribulation, or that it takes us to the very end of the Tribulation and the coming of the Lord in power to reign, it is immaterial *in relation to the subject before us.* In either event it seems quite evident that that which is described here is not the Rapture. It is a time of resurrection and woe, of vindication and wrath, of reward and judgment. Events similar to some of these occurrences will accompany the translation of the Church, but they are not identical events.

Those who are termed God's servants, or prophets, or saints in The Revelation, in chapters **6–19,** whose activities are obviously here on earth during the Tribulation, are not the Church but God's earthly people of that era—of the twelve tribes of Israel and out of every nation, kindred, people, and tongue (chap. **7**)—called His servants and saints as they have been since early creation. And we, God's people of this age, even though we do not agree on every detail in connection with the momentous predicted phenomena of the last days, may be united in giving glory to God as we read of the coming day when the kingdoms of this world will become the kingdom of our Lord, when He will take to Himself His great power and will reign. May God hasten that day!

CHAPTER XIV

THE CASTAWAYS AND THE OVERCOMERS

In Chapter I, we stated that we would examine the four viewpoints that prevail concerning the time of the translation of the Church in relation to the Tribulation: (1) Pre-Tribulationism, (2) Mid-Tribulationism, (3) Post-Tribulationism, and (4) Partial-Rapturism. The major points of argument of the first and third of these views have been discussed at some length. The second has been mentioned but once—in a single sentence. Nothing has been said about the fourth postulation to this time. It is fitting, therefore, that the second and fourth views should be considered in some degree.

Without any intent whatever to gloss over the position held by the mid-tribulationists, which is that the Rapture will take place at the sounding of the seventh trumpet which, they say, will be midway through the Tribulation, Daniel's Seventieth Week, their teaching stands or falls upon two factors: (1) the period of the Tribulation at which the seventh trumpet sounds; and (2) whether or not the last trump of I Corinthians 15:52 and the seventh trumpet of Revelation 11:15 are identical. Both of these problems have already been discussed at some length in Chapter XIII.

As to the period of the Tribulation at which the seventh trumpet is to sound, the weight of evidence appears to support the conclusion that it will be toward the end of Daniel's Seventieth Week rather than in the middle of it, Revelation 11:15–18 taking the reader as far, chronologically, as chapter 19:11–20:6. The kingdoms of this world becoming the kingdom of the Lord Jesus Christ, and His reigning; divine wrath wrought upon the angry nations; the rewarding, on earth, of

God's servants, the prophets, suggestive of Matthew 25:31ff—
these events intimate that the blowing of the seventh trumpet
will introduce the final overthrow of the enemies of Christ at
the end of this age and His initiatory acts at the beginning of
the Millennium.

It has been shown earlier, too, that the last trumpet to
sound a singular message for one people is not of necessity
coincident with the last of a series of trumpet-blasts carrying
a different message for a different people. The last trump of
I Corinthians 15:52, clearly identical with "the trump of God"
of I Thessalonians 4:16, has sufficient distinctive dissimilarities
to the seventh trumpet and the events that it institutes, to
make it extremely doubtful that the two are equivalent.

Consequently we allege that neither the period at which the
seventh trumpet is to sound nor its purport give convincing
support to the proposal that the translation of the Church will
be in the middle of the Tribulation. On the other hand, Scripture upon Scripture intimates that the Church will be per-
mitted to go through no part whatever of the Tribulation,
Daniel's Seventieth Week, a period during which God will be
dealing with the nation Israel once again rather than carrying
out His present activity of taking out of the Gentiles a people
for His name (Acts 15:14).

The theory of the partial-rapturists is not occupied so much
with the time of the translation of the Church in relation to the
Tribulation as it is with the identity of those who will be
translated. Partial-rapturists will not be found in the post-
tribulation school, inasmuch as there would be no reason for
them to suppose that only a select company of the Church will
be taken to be with Christ simply for the purpose of meeting
Him and returning with Him to the earth immediately. Most
of this school of thought holds the pre-tribulation view of the
Rapture, although a small minority will be found among the
mid-tribulationists.

It is the surmise of the partial-rapturists that there is a sort of spiritual aristocracy in the Church, composed of "overcomers," men and women who are especially devoted to the Lord and looking for His coming with great expectancy, who alone will be caught up to meet the Lord in the air when He comes for His own. This is a very brief summation of their position but it presents the gist of partial-rapturism.

Let it be said immediately that we have never known a single partial-rapturist who has not been a devoted and consecrated Christian. Believing, as they do, that the Lord has a "best" to offer to some of His saints, they long to experience it to the full and strive toward that goal which is, they affirm, to be numbered among the elect who will be caught up in the translation of the Church. As one very dear friend, now with the Lord, used to say: "I am almost thoroughly convinced that there will be two trains, and I want to be on the first." And his life gave ample evidence as to the reality of his desire.

It will not be necessary to set forth all of the points of argument that the partial-rapturists use. Four key citations will suffice: I Corinthians 9:24, 27; II Timothy 4:8; Hebrews 9:28; and Revelation 3:21. Suppose we examine them in order.

I Corinthians 9:24, 27: "Know ye not that they which run in a race run all, but one receiveth the prize? So run that ye may obtain. . . . But I keep under my body, and bring it into subjection: lest that by any means, when I have preached to others, I myself should be a castaway [lit., *rejected* or *disapproved*]." It is quite apparent that the Apostle Paul was speaking, not of salvation but of reward. Salvation is wholly by grace through faith, but our gracious God is pleased to reward His people for faithfulness in service. Paul therefore exhorted his readers so to run in this Christian life that they might obtain reward, and he declared that he himself was seeking to live in such a way that he would not be disapproved on account of lack of faithfulness and thus be rejected when the Lord should bestow His rewards. There is no evidence whatever, however, that the prize here denoted is that of being counted among a select company who will be raptured at the shout of the Lord.

II Timothy 4:8: "Henceforth there is laid up for me a crown of righteousness, which the Lord, the righteous judge, shall give me at that day: and not to me only, but unto all them also that love His appearing." Here a special reward is promised to all that are devoted to the appearing of the Lord. It will be a unique reward for a specific attitude of heart—"a crown of righteousness." It will be bestowed upon all who have exhibited love for Christ's coming, and it will be conferred *to all at one time,* that is, "at that day." "That day" is the day when "we must all appear before the judgment seat of Christ; that every one may receive the things done in his body, according to that he hath done, whether it be good or bad" (II Cor. 5:10). Other rewards will be awarded at the same time—crowns of rejoicing (I Thess. 2:19), life (Jas. 1:12, Rev. 2:10), glory (I Pet. 5:4), etc. Hence the reward for loving Christ's appearing cannot be participation in the Rapture, since all believers in Him will receive their individual crowns coincidentally. The "crown of righteousness [to be given] unto all them also that love His appearing," must be a glorious crown, an earnestly-to-be-desired reward from the Saviour's hand, but it will not be separation, in translation, from other members of Christ's body.

Hebrews 9:28: "So Christ was once offered to bear the sins of many; and unto them that look for Him shall He appear the second time without sin [sin apart] unto salvation." This is a text that, if taken by itself, might be considered firm ground for the partial-rapture theory. However, it is not generally the Spirit's way to teach doctrine by one sentence read apart from its context and without regard to other Scriptures. "Whom shall He make to understand doctrine? . . . For precept must be upon precept, precept upon precept; line upon line, line upon line; here a little, and there a little" (Isa. 28:9, 10). Thus we must examine this text in its setting, consider to whom it was specifically addressed, and compare it with other Scriptures if we are to know the whole truth of the matter.

The Lord Jesus Christ came to earth once for the distinct purpose of giving His life as a ransom for many, to bear their sins. By His death on the cross He purchased salvation for all, and all who come to Him in faith are born anew by the Holy Spirit. But Christ is coming to earth again, and this time it will be "sin apart," that is, it will not be for the purpose of settling the sin question, which has been accomplished once for all. When He comes again it will be "unto salvation"—that which was wrought at Calvary will be crowned at His second advent when His own blood-purchased saints will receive their redemption bodies, bodies incorruptible and immortal (Mark 10:45; John 3:6–8; Heb. 7:27; Rom. 8:23; I Cor. 15:53).

Now this appearing of our Lord, "sin apart unto salvation," is said to be "unto them that look for Him." Will He come, then, only to those who are earnestly longing to see Him at that time? Here is a case where the background and context of Scripture may be seen to be of utmost importance. This epistle was written to Hebrew-Christians, to those who had come out of Judaism into Christianity. The writer demonstrates in this treatise the superiority of the new covenant to the old, showing how the shadows of the old economy are made reality in the new. His initial readers would be familiar with the Levitical ordinances and forms of worship. So it is that he illuminates what he has to say about Christ's coming in language that will call to mind the Mosaic tabernacle and Aaron's service on the day of atonement.

When the sacrificial blood was shed on that day, the high priest entered the Holy of holies, but not without the blood of the sacrifice for his own sins as well as for those of the people. The congregation waited without, in faith. They were aware that God had provided a way of access to Himself, and that it was by means of an offering that was acceptable to Him. The Israelites believed this. They accepted it by faith. But faith did not become sight, hope did not become reality until the high priest returned from the Holy of holies. Seeing him come out, they knew, their faith was confirmed in the matter, that the sacrifice was sufficient. Had it not been, Aaron would not have returned, for he would have been consumed in the presence of the holiness of Almighty God. So the congregation looked for the high priest's appearing. Doubtless they did not all watch with equal intensity or appreciation. Some may have stood in the court with varying emotions and seeming lack of interest. Others may have been occupied in their thoughts with the mundane things of every day life. Yet unquestionably they all looked for him and, when he appeared, they breathed easier and rejoiced that their sins were covered and they had been received, in the person of their representative, as being judicially righteous.

Just so God's waiting saints, the Church, look for the Lord Jesus Christ today—all of them. Some may have higher, more devoted, more deeply spiritual expectancy than others. But all His own look for Him to appear. We know now that salvation is ours because of the cross and the empty tomb. We accept it in faith. But one day the Lord Jesus, our great High Priest, will come again apart from sin unto salvation. Then faith will become sight, indeed; our hope will become reality as we are united with Him and are like Him in His perfection, sharers of His glory. All the saints are looking for Him, but oh, how we ought to *long* to see Him! May the zeal for His coming, our longing for *Him,* increase as we see the day approaching.

In pursuance of this thought, I Thessalonians 5:9, 10, already cited in another connection, gives rather conclusive answer to the partial-rapture theory: "For God hath not appointed us to wrath, but to obtain salvation by our Lord Jesus Christ, who died for us, that, whether we wake or sleep, we should live together with Him." It is the clause, "whether we wake or sleep," that begs attention in this instance.

The word rendered "sleep" here (also in vss. 6, 7) is *katheudoo,* which carries not only the meaning *to sleep* but *to lie asleep, to sleep away one's life, to lie idle.* It is used, for example, in Matthew 26:45, where our Lord told His unwatchful disciples: "Sleep on now, and take your rest: behold, the hour is at hand, and the Son of man is betrayed into the hands of sinners." It is quite a different word from that which is translated "sleep" in I Thessalonians 4:14, namely, *koimaoo.* This latter word has the connotation *to sleep in death,* and it is so employed, not only in chapter 4 but also in Matthew 27:52; John 11:11-14; I Corinthians 11:30; and 15:51.

It is not by chance but by design that the Holy Spirit caused the Apostle Paul to make use of distinctive verbs in I Thessalonians 4 and 5, lest his readers might suppose that, in 5:10, he was alluding, in the expression "whether we wake or sleep," to the fact that both those who are living when Christ comes and those who have died in faith, will live together with Him. Indeed, they will! But the apostle's teaching here is that *all* believers, whether they be watchful, looking in earnest expectancy for His coming, or unwatchful and, perhaps, idle and slothful, will yet be taken into His presence when He comes. Why? Because not only our salvation but our translation also is entirely of grace—not earned but bestowed. All His own will live together with Him.

While, then, Hebrews 9:28 gives the partial-rapturists a seemingly strong talking point, its real meaning, combined with other Scriptures that declare a full translation of all the saints at one time, reveals that their theory is erroneous.

Revelation 3:21: "To him that overcometh will I grant to sit with Me in My throne, even as I also overcame, and am set down with My Father in His throne." It is in an effort, it appears, to understand who the overcomers of Revelation 2 and 3 are, that the partial-rapturists suggest them to be a select company of the Church who will be raptured apart from the remnant of the Church and granted the privilege of sitting upon Christ's throne. Such reasoning does not have scriptural support.

Other overcomers are mentioned in the letters to the seven churches in Asia, and to them, for example, it is said that it will be granted that they will eat of the tree of life (2:7), not be hurt of the second death (2:11), be given to eat of hidden manna and have new names (2:17), etc. Surely all these over-comers are equally to share in the Rapture! Can any believer in Christ be excluded from the promise that he "shall not be hurt of the second death"? The second death will take only those whose names are not written in the book of life (Rev. 20:11–15). Just as all Christians will share in this promise, in like manner none will be excluded from that of chapter 3:21. *All* the members of Christ's body, and not a chosen few, will sit with Him in His throne.

Who are the overcomers, then? Are they those Christians who have attained heights of spirituality that most of us will never know on this earth? The answer to their identity is found in I John 5:4, 5: "For whosoever is born of God over-cometh the world: and this is the victory that overcometh the world, even our faith. Who is he that overcometh the world, but he that believeth that Jesus is the Son of God?" The over-comer is he who triumphs by faith, faith in the Lord Jesus Christ as the Son of God and his own personal Saviour. By Him we overcome the world and Satan, the prince of this world today, overcoming him by the blood of the Lamb (Rev. 12:11). This includes all believers in Christ and not a special company of them. The messages to the overcomers cannot be construed as teaching a partial rapture of the Church.

Salvation is by grace through faith, and not of works (Eph. 2:8, 9). Scripture upon Scripture can be marshaled to prove this majestic truth. There is absolutely nothing a man can do to merit or earn one infinitesimal portion of his justification before God. As Dr. Pettingill used to say: "Salvation is by grace through faith—*plus nothing*."

The translation of the Church is not reward but is part and parcel of salvation. Moreover, our salvation will not be complete until we receive our redemption bodies, as we have seen (Rom. 8:23). That will not be until the Church is raptured. Consequently the key verse of many partial-rapturists works to the disadvantage of their teaching, for Christ's appearing is said to be, in Hebrews 9:28, "unto salvation." And if it be unto salvation, which is by grace through faith, how can it be earned as a reward? That would make salvation of works, and this is contrary to Scripture from beginning to end.

Furthermore, it is evident that prior to our Lord's return to earth in power and glory, when He will overthrow His enemies and rule in righteousness and peace, the marriage supper of the Lamb will take place (Rev. 19:7–10). This must be after the translation of the Church, obviously, else there would be no bride at the marriage supper, a strange phenomenon indeed. Is the divine bridegroom, whose wife is said to have made herself ready, to sit at the marriage supper with an imperfect bride, a wife mutilated and incomplete? Will there be a full component of guests there, the friends of the bridegroom (vs. 9), but only a partial bride? God forbid!—and His grace will forbid.

With due brotherly esteem, therefore, of saintly men of God who hold to the positions discussed in this chapter, we must conclude that neither the mid-tribulationists nor the partial-rapturists can substantiate with Scripture the teachings that they advance. We are all one, however, in this—our redemption is based upon the precious blood of Christ shed for us; our present life is in His life at the right hand of the throne of God; and our hope is set upon Him for whom we earnestly watch, "the Bright and Morning Star."

CHAPTER XV

CONCLUSION

Our examination of the Scriptures that relate to the subject under discussion is completed. It has not been exhaustive, for there are untouched portions of Holy Writ that might have been woven into the pattern, as, for example, typology in the Old Testament. Nevertheless all of those Scriptures which might be termed "the disputed passages" have been fully analyzed in, we trust, an honorable and fair manner.

It would be foolish not to admit that there are certain difficulties in reaching the true interpretation. Were this not so there would be no room for differences of opinion that are now held by godly men. It is our conclusion, however, that the Scriptures as a whole support the interpretation that the translation of the saints, the rapture of the Church, will occur before any portion of the Tribulation, Daniel's Seventieth Week, takes place. And it is our further conviction that, once the truth of this is seen, all difficulties vanish and all the Scriptures that pertain to the subject fall into place in such a way as to complete a perfectly clear and beautifully concise picture of God's dealing with His Church in wondrous grace in every phase of her redemption and union with Himself.

It is appropriate, as we draw this treatise to a close, to repeat what has been stated earlier: that diverse views concerning what the Scriptures teach, as to the time of the translation of the Church in relation to the Tribulation, do not involve heresy. Our fellowship with our brethren in Christ is not in the order of eschatological events but in the crucified, risen, ascended, and seated Son of God, our Lord Jesus Christ, who is coming again for His blood-bought saints, and with them also, to judge and to reign. Together we long to behold Him in all His beauty and to see Him vindicated and glorified in this world that once rejected Him and has since despised Him. God hasten the day!

When we are in glory with Christ, we shall discover which of us were correct in our interpretation, and which were mistaken—and there will be some in both categories! But while we wait for His coming, for *Him,* all of us—post-tribulationists, mid-tribulationists, partial-rapturists, and pre-tribulationists—are united, surely, in seeking earnestly to guard the unity of the Spirit in the bond of peace, forbearing one another in love (Eph. 4:2, 3), and looking for that blessed hope, and the appearing of the glory of our great God and Saviour Jesus Christ; "who gave Himself for us, that He might redeem us from all iniquity, and purify unto Himself a peculiar people, zealous of good works" (Tit. 2:13, 14). So let us live in this expectancy, soberly, righteously, and godly in this present dark and evil age.

THE END